Hebrews: Better Things

Hebrews: Better Things

Volume Two

A Commentary on Hebrews 9-13

By Daniel L. Segraves

Hebrews: Better Things

Volume Two
A Commentary on Hebrews 9-13

by Daniel L. Segraves

©1997, Word Aflame Press
Hazelwood, MO 63042-2299

Scripture quotations in this book are from the King James Version of the Bible unless otherwise identified. Scriptures noted NKJV are from The New King James Bible, Copyright 1990 Thomas Nelson Inc., Publishers.

Printed in United States of America

Printed by

Library of Congress Cataloging-in-Publication Data

Segraves, Daniel L., 1946—
    Hebrews : Better Things / by Daniel L. Segraves.
        p.   cm.
    Includes bibliographical references.
    Contents: v. 1. A commentary on Hebrews, 1-8 — v. 2. A commentary on Hebrews, 9-13.
    ISBN 1-56722-189-0 (v. 1). — ISBN 1-56722-188-2 (v. 2)
    1. Bible. N.T. Hebrews—Commentaries.   I. Title
    BS 2775.3.S44 1996
    222'.87077—dc20   96-36070
                                                CIP

Contents

Preface

Every New Testament epistle was written to address a specific issue or issues that arose in the first-century church. Some appear to be written to audiences almost exclusively Gentile (e.g., I and II Corinthians, Galatians, Ephesians, I and II Thessalonians), others to both Gentile and Jewish readers (e.g., Romans, Philippians), and still others to audiences almost exclusively Jewish (e.g., Hebrews, James).

The Book of Hebrews, as the name implies, was apparently written to deal with a tendency among some first-century Jewish Christians to defect to Judaism. We should not think, however, that this makes the book any less relevant to Gentile Christians living two millennia later. Throughout the Christian era, misunderstanding of the law of Moses (i.e., the old or Sinaitic covenant) and its relationship to the new covenant has been persistent, even among Gentiles. In some cases, this has led to Gentile believers embracing part or all of the law as normative for Christians. But the Book of Hebrews joins the Pauline epistles (e.g., Romans, Galatians, Ephesians, Colossians) in declaring the termination of all the Sinaitic covenant in favor of the new covenant established in Christ's blood. (See Hebrews 7:12, 18; 8:6, 7, 13; 10:9.)

The Book of Hebrews is Scripture inspired of God, and it is thus profitable for doctrine, for reproof, for correction, and for instruction in righteousness. (See II Timothy 3:16.) Its message harmonizes with and strengthens the

11

teaching of the other books of Scripture on every subject it touches.

Many commentaries have been written on the Book of Hebrews throughout the history of Christianity. Little has been written, however, from the perspective of Oneness Pentecostal theology. This work is intended to be an analysis and exegesis of the text, not simply an attempt to defend a denominational view. The exaltation of Christ so apparent in the book does, however, take on rich new significance when seen through the theology harmonious with all Scripture has to say on this subject: Jesus Christ is nothing less than God Himself revealed in a complete and authentic human being.

This commentary is based on the King James Version (KJV) of the Holy Bible. Where the wording of the KJV may tend to obscure the meaning for some modern readers, the reading of the New King James Version (NKJV) will be consulted. Where the critical Greek text (as seen in Nestle-Aland's 26th edition and the 3rd edition of the United Bible Societies' Greek New Testament) has a significantly different reading than the text upon which the NKJV and KJV are based, it will be discussed.

For fourteen years, I have taught a course in systematic theology that focuses on the termination of the old covenant and the establishment of a radically new covenant by Jesus Christ in His blood. This new covenant is superior in every way to the law given to Moses at Sinai. And this is the central message of the Book of Hebrews.

H.

The Heavenly Tabernacle Is Superior to the Earthly (9:1-28)

1. The Levitical Priesthood (9:1-10)

(1) Then verily the first covenant had also ordinances of divine service, and a worldly sanctuary. (2) For there was a tabernacle made; the first, wherein was the candlestick, and the table, and the shewbread; which is called the sanctuary. (3) And after the second veil, the tabernacle which is called the Holiest of all; (4) which had the golden censer, and the ark of the covenant overlaid round about with gold, wherein was the golden pot that had manna, and Aaron's rod that budded, and the tables of the covenant; (5) and over it the cherubims of glory shadowing the mercy seat; of which we cannot now speak particularly. (6) Now when these things were thus ordained, the priests went always into the first tabernacle, accomplishing the service of God. (7) But into the second went the high priest alone once every year, not without blood, which he offered for himself, and for the errors of the people: (8) the Holy Ghost this signifying, that the way into the holiest of all was not yet made manifest, while as the first tabernacle was yet standing: (9) which

was a figure for the time then present, in which were offered both gifts and sacrifices, that could not make him that did the service perfect, as pertaining to the conscience; (10) which stood only in meats and drinks, and divers washings, and carnal ordinances, imposed on them until the time of reformation.

Verse 1. The covenant God established with Israel at Mount Sinai featured "ordinances of divine service," but it was characterized by an "earthly sanctuary" (NKJV). The specific directions that God gave Moses for the construction of the Tabernacle begin in Exodus 25. The Tabernacle was simply a tent that served as a place for God to dwell among the Israelites. (See Exodus 25:8.)

The word translated "ordinances" (*dikaiomata*) comes from the same stem as the words translated "righteous" and "just." Because of the association of these ordinances with God, they are considered "divine" service. Romans 9:4 uses the same word translated "service" here (*latreias*) for "the service of God" associated with the giving of the law. This service consisted of the rituals related to the Tabernacle and Temple worship. It had to do exclusively with Israel, for it sprang from the law of Moses. The word translated "sanctuary" is *hagion*, forms of which are elsewhere translated "holy," "sanctify," and "saints." The essence of the concept of holiness is separation, and the Tabernacle was the ultimate holy place on earth because of its separation unto God and from all that was ritually unclean. This "holiness" was reinforced by severe penalties for those who defiled the sanctuary. (See Leviticus 10:1-3; 16:1-2; II Chronicles 26:16-23.)

But for all its holiness, the sanctuary of the first

covenant (the law of Moses) was nevertheless an earthly (*kosmikon*, from *kosmos*) structure. Thus it was not the "true tabernacle" (8:2) or the "heavenly thing" (8:5). As long as the covenant which focused on this earthly Tabernacle was in effect, "the way into the Holiest of All was not yet made manifest" (9:8, NKJV). The Tabernacle itself and the rituals associated with it were symbolic of a greater reality (9:9-10). There was a "greater and more perfect tabernacle" to come, not constructed by human beings (9:11). That the sanctuary accompanying the law of Moses was earthly indicates the inferiority of the old covenant to the new covenant, which features a heavenly ministry (9:23-25).

The significance of the Tabernacle as a symbol for greater things to come is seen in that fifty chapters in the Bible deal specifically with instructions relating to its construction and rituals: thirteen chapters in Exodus, eighteen in Leviticus, thirteen in Numbers, two in Deuteronomy and four in Hebrews. The importance of the Tabernacle is evident in that the Bible devotes only two chapters to the creation of the universe.

Verse 2. The earthly Tabernacle was thirty cubits long, approximately ten cubits wide and ten cubits high.[1] (A cubit is approximately 18 inches.) (See Exodus 26:15-28.) It was divided into two compartments. The first, the Holy Place, was twenty cubits long. In this compartment was the lampstand and the table of showbread. (See Exodus 25:23-39; 27:20-21; 37:10-24.)

We typically speak of the Tabernacle as a single structure, and so it was. But it actually consisted of two tents joined by strategically placed clasps.[2] The KJV translates the Greek more literally here than the NKJV: "For there was a tabernacle made; the first, wherein was the candle-stick, and the table, and the shewbread; which is called the sanctuary. And after the second veil, the tabernacle which is called the Holiest of all" (verses 2-3, KJV). Here we see two tabernacles, the sanctuary (or the Holy Place, *hagia*), and the Holiest of All (*hagia hagion*). The NKJV and some other translations supply the word "part," which is not found in the Greek text, into order to pre-serve the idea of a single sanctuary: "For a tabernacle was prepared: the first *part* . . . and behind the second veil, the part of the tabernacle" (verses 2-3, NKJV). It seems better to accept the reading of the KJV because the Greek text does not contain the extra word, adding the word obscures the clear meaning of the text, and from the Hebrew Scriptures we can establish the concept of two tents merged so as to form one. (See Exodus 26:6, 11; 36:13, 18.)

In that in the original Tabernacle, there was apparent-ly another piece of furniture in the Holy Place: the altar of incense. (See Exodus 30:1-10; 37:25-28; Leviticus 16:12, 18-20.) It is difficult to explain why the writer of Hebrews did not include the altar in his inventory of the furnish-ings in the Holy Place. Though there is limited manu-script evidence for including a reference to the altar of incense in this verse,[3] the overwhelming textual evidence excludes it. A further complication is that verse 4 seems to identify the "golden censer" as belonging to the Holiest of All behind the veil. Many translations render the Greek words *chrysoun thymiaterion* as "golden altar" rather than "golden censer."[4]

As we shall see in our examination of verse 4, this problem may resolve itself if we pay special attention to the writer's precise choice of words as it pertains to the "golden altar," which seems to be the preferred translation. In any event, the silence of verse 2 on the subject of the altar of incense is no proof it was not in the Holy Place; the writer of this letter obviously had his own reasons for not referring to this piece of furniture in conjunction with the lampstand and the table of showbread. He did not deny the presence of the altar of incense in the Holy Place; he simply did not mention it.

It is common to see the lampstand as symbolic of Jesus Christ the light of the world and the showbread as symbolic of Jesus the bread of life.[5] This symbolism may very well be true, but the Book of Hebrews develops neither theme. Indeed, after mentioning four of the main pieces of furniture in the Tabernacle, the writer remarked, "Of these things we cannot now speak in detail" (verse 5, NKJV). The purpose of this section of Hebrews is not to explore in minute detail all the symbolism inherent in the Tabernacle, but to focus on the more narrow range of symbolism found in the way the blood of animals offered once each year on the Day of Atonement represented the blood of Jesus (verses 7-14).

The practical function of the seven-branched lampstand, which stood on the south side of the sanctuary, was to illuminate perpetually the interior of the Holy Place. (See Exodus 27:20-21; Leviticus 24:2-4.) Each Sabbath, twelve freshly baked cakes of bread were placed on the table of showbread,[6] which stood on the north side of the sanctuary. (See Exodus 40:22.) The cakes were eaten by the priests and replaced. (See Exodus 25:23-30; 37:10-16; Leviticus 24:5-9.)

Some have suggested a symbolism more immediate to

national Israel. In this view, the twelve cakes of show-bread symbolized "God's provision for the 12 tribes of Israel" and the lampstand symbolized "the continuing witness of the covenant community (Zec 4:1-7; Rv 2:1)."[7]

Verse 3. The Holy Place was separated from the Holiest of All by "the second veil." (See Exodus 26:31-35; 36:35-36.) It is called the "second veil" to differentiate it from the first veil, which screened the entrance into the Tabernacle. (See Exodus 26:36-37; 36:37-38.) The area behind the second veil was called the Holiest of All or the Most Holy Place (verse 12) because it was the one place on earth most separated unto God and from all else. Although the Holy Place was separated unto God and from the bulk of people in Israel, any qualified priest could enter it to perform the ritual service. But only the high priest could enter the Most Holy Place, and then only once each year on the Day of Atonement (verse 7; Leviticus 16).

This second veil was torn apart in the Temple at Jerusalem at the time of Christ's death. (See Matthew 27:51.) This event was a dramatic and undeniable signal that the law of Moses was terminated. It was a divine signal, for the veil was torn without human intervention from top to bottom. According to Jewish tradition, the veil was four inches thick and was so strong it could not be torn by teams of oxen pulling in opposite directions.

The veil was apparently a symbol of the genuine humanity of the Messiah (10:19-20). His death on the cross dealt with the sin problem so completely and finally that it removed the barrier between God and humanity and made a way for all people to come directly into the presence of God.

The translation of the KJV is preferable here: "And after the second veil, the tabernacle which is called Holiest of all." This rendering preserves the idea in the Greek text that, in a sense, there were two tents connected in such a way as to form one.[8] The NKJV offers this translation: "And behind the second veil, the part of the tabernacle which is called the Holiest of All." But there is no basis in the Greek text for the words "part of the."

Verse 4. In contrast to the discussion of the Holy Place and its contents in verse 2, the discussion now turns to the Holiest of All. The reference to the "golden censer" is problematic for the following reasons: (1) There is no evidence from the Hebrew Scriptures that a golden censer (a shallow pan for the burning of incense) was permanently housed in the Most Holy Place. The high priest was to take a censer full of burning coals into the Most Holy Place on the Day of Atonement and burn incense there before the Mercy Seat (Leviticus 16:12-13), but Scripture gives no indication as to where this censer was permanently kept. Nor do the Hebrew Scriptures ever refer to the censer used by the high priest as a "golden" censer.[9] (2) The translation "golden altar" is probably better, in which case it refers to the altar of incense, which was overlaid with gold. But according to the Pentateuch, it was located within the Holy Place, not the Most Holy Place. It was placed just outside the veil that separated the two compartments, so that it was the item of furniture closest to the ark of the covenant, but it was not in the compartment with the ark. (See Exodus 30:1-10; 37:25-28.)

We can resolve the problem by noting that verse 4 does not say that the golden censer (altar) was *in* the

Holiest of All, but that the Most Holy Place *had* the golden altar. That is, the altar of incense was associated intimately with the ark of the covenant by its use; it pertained to the ark by virtue of the rituals performed on the Day of Atonement. (See Leviticus 16:12-20; Exodus 30:10.) Incense is generally thought to symbolize worship (Malachi 1:11) and prayer (Psalm 141:2; Revelation 8:3-4), because it is "something that ascended from a sacrifice, a pleasing aroma to God."[10] As it pertains to the ministry of Jesus, the altar of incense is thought to symbolize His intercession for human beings.[11]

The incense itself was made from a special recipe to be used exclusively on the altar of incense. If anyone attempted to duplicate the formula for personal use, he would be "cut off from his people" (Exodus 30:34-38, NKJV). This instruction further emphasizes the holiness of the things associated with the worship of God in the Tabernacle; they were to be kept separate from common use.

The item of furniture that was unquestionably within the Holiest of All was the ark of the covenant. (See Exodus 25:10-22; 37:1-5; Leviticus 16:2; I Kings 8:6.) The ark was a box overlaid with gold, and it originally contained three things: a golden pot in which manna was supernaturally preserved (Exodus 16:32-34), the rod of Aaron that budded supernaturally to indicate that God had chosem him and his sons to serve as priests (Numbers 16; 17:1-11), and the two tablets of stone upon which the Ten Commandments were written (Exodus 34:29; Deuteronomy 10:1-5). By the time the ark of the covenant was placed into the Most Holy Place of Solomon's Temple, however, all that remained in it were the tables of stone. (See I Kings 8:9.) Any attempt to

locate the manna or Aaron's rod after that point is speculation.

It is significant that the tablets of the Ten Commandments were called "the tablets of the covenant" (NKJV).
For all practical purposes, the law of Moses was itself the
covenant. (See Deuteronomy 10:8.) Thus, it is the law of
Moses that has been made obsolete (8:13) and that has
been replaced by the new covenant (8:6-12).

Verse 5. On top of the ark of the covenant were two
cherubim, or angels, fashioned from one solid piece of
gold together with the mercy seat. (See Exodus 25:17-22;
37:6-9; Leviticus 16:2, 13-15.) The mercy seat was a flat
slab toward which the cherubim faced in a symbol of
angelic protection,[12] for it was upon the mercy seat that
the presence of God descended to meet with the high
priest. (See Exodus 25:22; Psalm 80:1; 99:1.) On the Day
of Atonement, the high priest sprinkled blood upon the
mercy seat to atone for the sins of the people of Israel.
(See Leviticus 16:14-34.)

The term "mercy seat," which was first entered into
English translations by William Tyndale, comes from the
Hebrew verb *kapporeth*, which means "to make atonement," in the sense of covering sin. In the Greek text of
the New Testament, the word translated "mercy seat" is
hilasterion. The same word is translated "propitiation"
in Romans 3:25 in reference to the blood of Christ, and
another form of the word (*hilasmos*) is found in I John
2:2; 4:10, also in reference to the way the blood of Jesus
satisfies the righteous judgment of God on the sins of
the human race. We can therefore safely say that the
blood sprinkled upon the mercy seat by the high priest
under the old covenant was a symbol of the blood of the

Lamb of God, Jesus Christ, who would take away the sin of the world (John 1:29, 36). Verses 7-15 reinforce this symbolism.

Regarding the golden censer (altar), it may seem problematic to say that the verb "had" (*echousa*) refers to its association with the Holiest of All rather than demanding its location within the Most Holy Place, because the same verb serves to locate the ark of the covenant. But it "would not be impossible for such a common term . . . to be used in different senses in relation to its two direct objects."[13] Since the testimony of Scripture elsewhere is abundantly clear in describing the altar of incense as being located in the Holy Place and the ark of the covenant as residing in the Most Holy Place, that must be its meaning here. The writer of such a book as Hebrews would certainly have known the details of the Tabernacle, as would his original readers. We must seek to understand this reference in the same way as they would have understood it.

Even though the previous verses have described in some detail the contents of the Holy Place, the Most Holy Place, and the ark of the covenant, verse 5 declares, "Of these things we cannot now speak in detail" (NKJV). It was not the purpose of the author to enter into a lengthy discussion of the minutiae of the Tabernacle. As significant and great as the Tabernacle was, it had served its purpose and was now obsolete. (See 8:13.) The purpose of this letter was not to encourage the original readers in their renewed fascination with the law of Moses, but to point them to the greater reality of which the law was only a shadow. The greatest and most significant symbolism provided by the law was its foreshadowing of the way in which the blood of Jesus would gain immediate access for all people into the very presence of God. (See verses 7-15.) That is what the Book of Hebrews discusses in detail.

Verse 6. After the construction of the Tabernacle (Exodus 40), including the building of each item of furniture (Exodus 36-39), the priests "always" went into the Holy Place, the first compartment. (See comments on verse 2.) The point is that entry into the Holy Place was not as restricted as entry into the Most Holy Place (verse 7). Any qualified priest could enter the Holy Place, and priests entered it daily as they performed their duties. These duties included tending the lampstand and burning incense (Exodus 27:20-21; 30:7-8; Leviticus 24:1-4). Weekly the showbread was set out (Leviticus 24:8-9). (On the word "service," see comments on verse 1.)

As in verse 2, the Greek text here indicates not that the priests went into the first *part* of the Tabernacle, as suggested by the NKJV, but into the *first Tabernacle*, as accurately translated by the KJV. (See comments on verses 2-3.) Although, in the final analysis, there was only one Tabernacle formed from the joining of the two tents together by the golden clasps just above the veil that hung down to separate the Holy Place from the Most Holy Place, the linen canopy that was the first covering placed over the Tabernacle framework was actually two canopies that were not sewn together. (See Exodus 26:1-6.) In one sense, they were joined by the golden clasps, but in another sense, they were kept separate by the same clasps, because the fabric itself was not integrated. The same was true with the canopy of goats' hair that covered the linen canopy. It was made up of two canopies joined by bronze clasps. (See Exodus 26:7-13.)

Thus, the sanctity of the Most Holy Place was pre-served. Although the high priest passed directly from the Holy Place into the Most Holy Place, the Most Holy Place was separated by a veil and by the golden and bronze clasps. (See comments on verse 3.)

Verse 7. In contrast to the relatively free access that qualified priests had into the Holy Place, only the high priest could enter the Most Holy Place in the Tabernacle, and he could enter it only once each year, on the Day of Atonement. (See Leviticus 16.) We should understand the high priest's entrance into the Most Holy Place "once a year" (NKJV) as referring to one day a year, for he actually entered it at least twice on the Day of Atonement.

It was required that he bring blood with him as he entered. First, he had to sprinkle the blood of a bull upon the mercy seat to make atonement for himself and the members of his house. (See Leviticus 16:3, 6, 11, 14.) Then, after exiting the Most Holy Place, he had to kill a goat and reenter the Most Holy Place to sprinkle its blood on the mercy seat for the sins of the people. (See Leviticus 16:15-16.) He may actually have entered three times, with the first being to put in place the "censer full of burning coals" on which incense burned to obscure the mercy seat from his vision (Leviticus 16:12-13). Jewish tradition suggests there were four entries into the Most Holy Place, with the final one being to retrieve the equipment first taken in for the burning of incense at the beginning of the ceremony.[14]

After the high priest concluded the ceremony in the Most Holy Place, he returned to the Holy Place and sprinkled some of the blood of the bull and goat on the Altar of Incense. (See Leviticus 16:18.) While this annual ceremo-

24

ny was conducted, no other priest could enter the Tabernacle. (See Leviticus 16:17.) Since the events of the Day of Atonement were symbolic of a far greater reality (verse 9)—the ultimate and final atonement provided by Christ (verses 11-15)—the restriction of both the Holy Place and the Most Holy Place to the high priest alone may represent the exclusivity of Christ's sacrifice. No one else participated in it. True cleansing from sin does not come by the work of Christ Jesus and someone else, but by His work alone.

The reference to "sins committed in ignorance" (NKJV) indicates that human beings are responsible for all their sins, even those committed unknowingly. The proverbial saying "ignorance is bliss" is certainly not accurate theologically. Whether or not a person is fully aware of his responsibilities to God, he is accountable for his failure to adhere to those responsibilities. (See Luke 12:48.) The law of Moses prescribed specific sacrifices for sins knowingly committed (e.g., Leviticus 6:1-7), though for some intentional sins there was apparently no recourse (e.g., Numbers 15:30-31). In addition to the general cleansing on the Day of Atonement for sins committed in ignorance, the law made other provisions for cleansing from such sins, apparently if they were discovered after the fact to be sin. (See Numbers 15:22-29.) It seems the sacrifice of the Day of Atonement dealt with every infraction of the law that had not been dealt with previously throughout the year by other sacrifices.

Two aspects of the good news of the gospel are pertinent here: (1) Since He was sinless, Christ did not need to offer a sacrifice for Himself (4:15; 7:26-27). (2) The blood of Jesus atones not just for sins committed in ignorance, but for all sins, even those committed deliberately (9:26; John 1:29; I John 2:2). His sacrifice is thus immeasurably superior to even that of the Day of Atonement. There can be no limit to the efficacy of Christ's blood, for His death was of infinite value.

Verse 8. What the Holy Spirit intended to signify by the rituals of the Day of Atonement is that the way into the true "Holiest of All was not yet made manifest while the first Tabernacle was still standing" (NKJV). (See verses 11-12.) As dramatic as the events of the Day of Atonement were, they were mere symbols of a greater reality. (See verses 9, 23-24.) The ceremonies served to illustrate not how simple and easy it was to gain access into the immediate presence of God, but how difficult it was. Nothing about the Day of Atonement suggested to the people of Israel that they too could enjoy intimate fellowship with God. Instead, the rituals were frightening and exclusive. The high priest entered the Most Holy Place at the risk of his own death. Jewish tradition indicates that the prayer of the high priest when he exited the Most Holy Place was intentionally short "lest he put Israel in terror." When he survived the last ritual and the day was over, he invited his friends to a feast in celebration.[15]

The phrase "while the first tabernacle was still standing" further supports the claim of the author of Hebrews that the Tabernacle associated with the law of Moses was a thing of the past. (See comments on 8:13; 9:1.) At the time this book was written, it was no longer standing. It had, of course, been replaced by the Temple, but the author was not interested in the Temple standing in Jerusalem at the moment he wrote. It would soon be destroyed. He was interested in the original intent and function of Tabernacle worship as prescribed by Moses under the first covenant and its comparison to new covenant worship as prescribed by Jesus.

Verse 9. The Tabernacle and all its rituals were "symbolic for the present time" (NKJV). (See also 10:1; Colossians 2:16-17.) With the coming of the new covenant, this covenant of symbols had served its purpose (8:13). The gifts and sacrifices offered under the law of Moses were incapable of making him "who performed the service perfect in regard to the conscience" (NKJV). (See 10:1-2.) The point is that those ritual offerings provided no assurance of right standing with God. Since the blood of bulls and goats did not take away sin but merely served to remind Israel of their sinfulness (10:3-4), the sacrifices left the people of Israel with a troubled conscience. This does not mean that no one under the law ever enjoyed a clear conscience, but that no one obtained a clear conscience simply by the sacrificial rituals. During the law, people gained a clear conscience with God by faith in Him, just as today. (See 11:1-2, 6, 39.)

Verse 10. The sacrificial rituals of the law of Moses were external; they did not deal with the needs of the inner person. They pertained to "foods and drinks, various washings, and fleshly ordinances" (NKJV). (See 13:9.) Leviticus 11 details the laws concerning clean and unclean foods. There were also regulations concerning acceptable drinks in a variety of circumstances (Leviticus 10:8-9; 11:33-38; Numbers 6:2-3). Rules governed ceremonial washings that brought ritual cleansing (Exodus 30:20; Leviticus 15:4-27; 17:15-16; Numbers 19:7-13).

All of these regulations, and others like them in the law of Moses, were "fleshly" (NKJV). (See comments on

7:16.) The author of Hebrews did not use "flesh" (*sarx*) here, as Paul commonly did, to mean the sin nature.[16] He meant, rather, that the rituals of the law were external, pertaining to the outer person rather than the inner person.

In a telling statement supporting his previous declarations concerning the termination of the law of Moses with the coming of Messiah, the author declared that all of the ordinances of the law were "imposed until the time of reformation" (NKJV). A more literal translation of the Greek text at this point indicates that they were in force until the time of "setting things right" or "straight." Contextually, this time of "reformation" refers to the establishment of the new covenant (8:13; 9:11-15). This new covenant pertains to the inner person by cleansing the conscience (verse 14), giving full assurance of one's right standing with God.

2. The Priesthood of Christ
(9:11-14)

(11) But Christ being come an high priest of good things to come, by a greater and more perfect tabernacle, not made with hands, that is to say, not of this building; (12) neither by the blood of goats and calves, but by his own blood he entered in once into the holy place, having obtained eternal redemption for us. (13) For if the blood of bulls and of goats, and the ashes of an heifer sprinkling the unclean, sanctifieth to the purifying of the flesh: (14) how much more shall the blood of Christ, who through the eternal Spirit offered himself without spot to God, purge your con-

science from dead works to serve the living God?

Verse 11. In contrast to the temporary and symbolic ministry of the earthly Tabernacle and the Levitical priesthood, Jesus Christ is the great High Priest associated "with the greater and more perfect tabernacle not made with hands, that is, not of this creation" (NKJV). The Tabernacle built under Moses' direction was not the actual or final sanctuary. It merely represented something to come. The true Tabernacle is not built by men; it is otherworldly. (See comments on 8:2, 5; 9:1, 23.) Here again we see that the law of Moses and its rituals were never intended to be permanent; they were "imposed until the time of reformation" (9:10, NKJV), and that reformation was the termination of the old covenant and its replacement with the new covenant. (See 8:13.)

A textual variant here reads "the good things that have come" (Greek, *ton genomenon agathon*) as opposed to "the good things to come" (Greek, *ton mellonton agathon*). Both readings have substantial support from the Greek manuscripts. Metzger is of the opinion that the copyists who included the second reading may have been influenced by 10:1, where *ton mellonton agathon* appears without variant.[17] If the first reading is preferred, the idea is that with the coming of Christ and His high priestly ministry, the good things (i.e., the better covenant and promises [8:6]) have come; they are completely realized in Him. If the second reading is preferred, the point is that "Christ is High Priest . . . of the glorious future of hope."[18]

Verse 12. When Christ entered the true Most Holy Place, a reference to heaven itself as opposed to the inner sanctuary of the earthly Tabernacle (9:24), He went in with His own blood. (See 13:12 and Acts 20:28.) His blood stands in stark contrast to the blood of goats and calves with which the high priest entered under the law, and it demonstrates the superiority of the new covenant. All of the blood offered under the law was symbolic (9:8-9); it did not take away sin (10:4). The blood of animals was merely a pale shadow of the blood that would deal completely and finally with the sin problem: the blood of Jesus (10:1).

The entrance of Jesus into the true Most Holy Place was once for all, because by His blood He "obtained eternal redemption." This event brought to an end the law of Moses with its annual visits of the high priest into the earthly Holy of Holies. (See verses 7-8, 25-28; 10:10, 14.) Under the law, the blood of animals was shed repeatedly, but the blood of Jesus will never be offered again. (See Romans 6:10.) Since the death of Jesus was of infinite value, it obtained *eternal* redemption (cf. the "eternal Spirit" [verse 14] and the "eternal inheritance" [verse 15]).

The word translated "redemption" (Greek, *lutrosin*) has to do with making a ransom. It appears also in Luke 1:68; 2:38. Another form of the word (Greek, *apolutrosis*) appears elsewhere (e.g., Luke 21:28; Romans 3:24; Hebrews 9:15; 11:35). The blood of Jesus provided the payment necessary to satisfy the righteous judgment of God against sin.

Verse 13. The blood of bulls and goats refers to the sacrifices on the Day of Atonement. (See comments on verse 7.) The high priest first offered the blood of a bull for his own sins and the sins of his family, and then he offered the blood of a goat for the sins of the people.

The "ashes of a heifer" refers to the ritual under the law in which an unblemished red heifer was slaughtered outside the camp of Israel and then burned. Its ashes, when mixed with running water and sprinkled on an unclean person or thing, provided cleansing from ritual defilement. (See Numbers 19.)

The point is that these rituals provided sanctification merely "for the purifying of the flesh," or the outer person. (See comments on verse 10.) This is characteristic of the entire sacrificial system of the law of Moses. The uncleanness described in Numbers 19 is not moral, but ceremonial. It included the ritual uncleanness caused by touching a dead body or entering a tent where someone has died. The sacrifices of the law did not resolve the alienation from God caused by moral imperfection; they dealt only with external ceremonial uncleanness. "Christ's death met certain objectives and operated in a sphere different from that of the animal sacrifices of the old economy. . . . Animal sacrifices were efficacious in the sphere of ceremonial cleansing. They were not efficacious, however, in the realm of conscience and therefore in the matter of spiritual salvation. . . . Christ's offering is superior in that it accomplished something the Levitical offerings never could, namely, soteriological benefits."[19]

Verse 14. It would be a misstatement to say that the blood of Jesus was as effective in cleansing the conscience as the sacrifices of the law were in providing ceremonial cleansing for the outer person. We cannot equate the effect of Jesus' blood to anything else. It is more correct to say that if the sacrifices of the law provided ceremonial cleansing, "how much more" is the effect of the blood of Christ. That is, the blood of Christ is even more effective in cleansing from sin than the sacrifices of the law were in cleansing from ceremonial uncleanness. This is not to say that the sacrifices of the law were ineffective, but that the value of the blood of Jesus is infinite, so that when we compare it to anything else, only superlatives are appropriate. (See 8:6.)

Whereas the sacrifices of the law could not "make him who performed the service perfect in regard to the conscience" (9:9, NKJV), the blood of Jesus cleanses the conscience from "dead works." Given the right context, we might think that "dead works" (Greek, *nekron ergon*) refers to sins. Indeed, some translations render these words as "works that lead to death." But "dead works" is a more accurate and literal translation, and in this context the reference seems to be to the works of the law of Moses. (See comments on 6:6.) Though the blood of Jesus certainly does cleanse from sin (9:26, 28), included in that sin is defection from exclusive faith in Jesus Christ and rejection of the new covenant in favor of the old covenant. This was the temptation that the original readers of the Book of Hebrews faced. The works of the law were dead because, with their fulfillment in the person of Christ, their purpose was accomplished and they were terminated. (See Matthew 5:17-18.) Instead of focusing on rituals now dead, believers should focus on serving "the living God." Even though God gave Israel the law, He is above and beyond it; His existence is not in any way tied to or dependent upon the law. (See Matthew 12:8.) "The writer wished his readers would give up all thoughts of returning to Old-Covenant rituals. Their consciences ought to be perfectly free from any need to engage in such things and, retaining their confidence in the perfect efficacy of the Cross, they should hold fast their profession and serve the living God within the New-Covenant arrangements."[20]

Christ offered Himself to God "through the eternal Spirit." This statement demonstrates that God did not forsake the Messiah on the cross. We should understand His lament, "My God, My God, why have you forsaken Me?" (Matthew 27:46, NKJV), in the context of Psalm 22, from which He quoted it. It is a poetic expression of the aloneness the Messiah experienced in His human existence at the point of this ultimate crisis. The following words from Psalm 22:1 illuminate the meaning: "Why are You so far from helping Me, and from the words of My groaning?" (NKJV). Though the Messiah was divine as well as human, He was not spared any of the suffering associated with His substitutionary death. In His humanity, He accepted and felt the full brunt of the consequence of the sins He bore: alienation from God.

But there was not an actual separation of deity from humanity. If the Incarnation is genuine, such a thing could not be. Jesus was not a human person and a divine person both living in one body; He was one person, at once both human and divine. The statement that Christ offered Himself to God "through the eternal Spirit" means that "in the power of the Divine Spirit . . . that the Servant [Messiah] accomplishes every phase of his ministry, including the crowning phase in which he accepts death for the transgression of his people."[21] If the Spirit of God had withdrawn from Him on the cross, the Messiah would have been incapable of accomplishing eternity's greatest achievement, for He would have been no more than a man, though a sinless one. But Jesus did all He did in the power of the Spirit. (See Luke 4:14.) To suggest that He ever did anything apart from the Spirit of God would be to imply an untenable fracture between His humanity and deity. But at the same time, His deity did not overwhelm or eradicate His humanity to spare Him from the suffering associated with human existence, including the sense of alienation He experienced on the cross.

Jesus "offered Himself." His was a willing sacrifice. His life was not taken from Him; He laid it down. (See John 10:17-18.) At no point in Jesus' life, including the moment of His death, was Jesus the unwilling victim of Satan or people. Although people crucified Him, and although Satan was involved in engineering the circumstances surrounding the crucifixion (see Luke 22:3), God was completely in control, ensuring that everything that happened was according to His divine purpose. All Satan or humans could see was what was happening in the temporal realm. Had they known what the death of the Messiah would accomplish in the realm of the Spirit, they would not have carried it out. (See I Corinthians 2:7-8.)

Jesus was a sacrifice "without spot." Sacrifices under the law of Moses had to be without blemish (e.g., Exodus 12:5; 29:1; Leviticus 1:3, 10; 3:1, 6; 4:3.). Christ was spotless in that He was without sin (4:15; 7:26-27; Isaiah 53:9). In contrast to the high priest under the law of Moses, whose first sacrifice on the Day of Atonement dealt with his own uncleanness (verse 7), the sacrifice of Jesus was completely altruistic.

That Christ offered Himself to God does not suggest a multiplicity of persons within the Godhead. It is significant that throughout this passage, the writer referred to

"Christ" exclusively. (See 9:11, 14, 24, 28.) The English "Christ" is transliterated from the Greek *Christos*, which is the equivalent of the Hebrew *Messiach*, or Messiah. Both words mean "anointed one." Thus "Christ" is always a reference to His genuine humanity, which was anointed by the Holy Spirit. (See Luke 4:18.) The Book of Hebrews uses "Christ Jesus" once (3:1), "Jesus Christ" three times (10:10; 13:8, 21), "Jesus" nine times (2:9; 4:14; 6:20; 7:22; 10:19; 12:2, 24; 13:12), and "Christ" nine times (3:6, 14; 5:5; 6:1; 9:11, 14, 24, 28; 11:26). While there may not be a specific purpose in each use, it seems that "Christ Jesus" or "Christ" focuses on the genuineness of the Messiah's human nature, while "Jesus Christ" or "Jesus" focuses attention on the reality of His deity. ("Jesus" means "Yahweh-Savior" or "Yahweh is Salvation.")

In this verse, the Messiah offers Himself to God. Since the title of "Messiah" has to do with a human being anointed by God, the point is that as it pertained to His human nature, Christ willingly gave Himself as a sacrifice to God. (See Luke 23:46.) To suggest that "Christ" and "God" refer to two divine persons is problematic, for it suggests a separateness within God's identity so substantial that one intelligent person can meaningfully offer something to another intelligent person. Traditional trinitarianism defines God as "three distinct persons," but not as "three *separate and* distinct persons."[22] But if one divine person can offer something, including himself, to another divine person, some kind of radical separation is required. It is more contextually satisfying, and more in harmony with all the Scripture has to say concerning monotheism, to see this verse as meaning that the Messiah's offering sprang from the fullness and genuineness of His humanity.

3. The Blood of the Covenant
(9:15-28)

(15) And for this cause he is the mediator of the new testament, that by means of death, for the redemption of the transgressions that were under the first testament, they which are called might receive the promise of eternal inheritance. (16) For where a testament is, there must also of necessity be the death of the testator. (17) For a testament is of force after men are dead: otherwise it is of no strength at all while the testator liveth. (18) Whereupon neither the first testament was dedicated without blood. (19) For when Moses had spoken every precept to all the people according to the law, he took the blood of calves and of goats, with water, and scarlet wool, and hyssop, and sprinkled both the book, and all the people, (20) saying, This is the blood of the testament which God hath enjoined unto you. (21) Moreover he sprinkled with blood both the tabernacle, and all the vessels of the ministry. (22) And almost all things are by the law purged with blood; and without shedding of blood is no remission. (23) It was therefore necessary that the patterns of things in the heavens should be purified with these; but the heavenly things themselves with better sacrifices than these. (24) For Christ is not entered into the holy places made with hands, which are the figures of the true; but into heaven itself, now to appear in the presence of God for us: (25) nor yet

that he should offer himself often, as the high priest entereth into the holy place every year with blood of others; (26) for then must he often have suffered since the foundation of the world: but now once in the end of the world hath he appeared to put away sin by the sacrifice of himself. (27) And as it is appointed unto men once to die, but after this the judgment: (28) so Christ was once offered to bear the sins of many; and unto them that look for him shall he appear the second time without sin unto salvation.

Verse 15. By virtue of His death, Christ qualifies to be the mediator of the new covenant. (For a discussion of the significance of His role as mediator, see comments on 8:6.) The replacement of the old covenant with the new covenant is a major theme of Hebrews. (See 7:22; 8:6-10, 13; 9:1, 16-18, 20; 10:16, 29; 12:24; 13:20.) The chief characteristic of the new covenant is that, as opposed to the old covenant, it provides redemption from sin. (See 10:4.) Since the blood of animals could not deal with the sin problem, during the law of Moses God "passed over" the sins of the people (Romans 3:25, NKJV). He did not ignore their sins, but He reserved His judgment for the day when Jesus Christ would die on the cross for the sins of the world. Those who had faith in God were forgiven on the basis of the blood that Jesus would shed, just as people of faith in this era are forgiven on the basis of the blood Jesus has shed. (See 11:1-2, 6, 39; Revelation 13:8.)

The death of Jesus provided "redemption of the trans-gressions under the first covenant" (NKJV). (For a discussion of "redemption," see comments on verse 12.) The first covenant, the law of Moses established at Mount Sinai, did not provide redemption from sin. (See comments on verse 13.) As 9:10 and 13 indicate, "the Levitical offerings were related to 'food and drink and various washings, regulations for the body,' and the sprinkling of blood so as to sanctify and purify the flesh. Animal sacrifices were efficacious in removing ceremonial uncleanness."[23] They were not efficacious in removing moral uncleanness. For this reason they could not make anyone "perfect in regard to the conscience" (verse 9, NKJV). (See also 10:1-2.)

Redemption from sin was necessary so "that those who are called may receive the promise of the eternal inheritance" (NKJV). This statement explains the "promise" that the people of faith prior to the new covenant "did not receive," even though they "obtained a good testimony" (11:39, NKJV). References to eternal life under the old covenant are scarce and veiled. Only with the coming of the new covenant does the concept of eternal life spring with clear emphasis to the forefront.[24] The only clear reference to eternal life in the Old Testament is in Daniel 12:2. A more obscure reference is in Job 14:13-15; 19:25-26. But nowhere does the Old Testament suggest that people can gain eternal life simply by adherence to the law of Moses. The only "life" promised in return for adherence to the law was long life in the Promised Land. (See comments on 3:1.)[25]

"Those who are called" (NKJV) does not mean a limited number of people determined by a prior choice of the sovereign God. This view, as suggested by the Calvinistic doctrines of "unconditional election," "limited atonement," and "irresistible grace," cannot avoid the consequence that salvation is unavailable to some people and that the blood of Jesus is not adequate to atone for the sins of all humanity. The comprehensive teaching of the New Testament is that salvation is available to all who will trust in Jesus; His blood is of infinite value and is therefore sufficient to atone for the sins of the whole world. (See John 3:16; 7:37-39; Mark 16:15-16; I John 2:2; I Timothy 2:4; II Peter 3:9; Revelation 22:17.) All humanity is called to believe on Jesus; it is a universal appeal and obligation. But only those who partake "of the heavenly calling" (3:1) by putting their trust in Him actually receive the eternal inheritance.

The words "may receive" (NKJV) are translated from the Greek *labosin*, the aorist active subjunctive form of *lambano*. The subjunctive mood indicates that receiving the inheritance is potential, pending the meeting of certain conditions. In this case, the condition is faith in Jesus Christ. If "those who are called" (NKJV) meant an elect number who are predestined to salvation as opposed to the universal call to all humanity, it is difficult to see why the writer used the subjunctive mood. The subjunctive mood implies a condition and suggests that those who are called may *not* receive the promise if they do not meet the condition. But the Calvinistic vision holds that those who are called—an elect number out of the entire human populace—will without question be saved. If that were the point here, it seems that the indicative mood would have been used, for the indicative expresses action that is actually taking place.

The role of Christ's death in establishing the new covenant is addressed more fully in verses 16-28.

Verses 16-17. These verses describe the new covenant

39

established by the death of Christ (see Matthew 26:28) as His last will and testament. (For a discussion of the word *diatheke*, here translated "testament" and elsewhere "covenant," see comments on 7:22.) In order for a will or testament to be in effect, the death of the one making the testament is necessary. The new covenant required only the death of Jesus Christ to be established. Just as a human being draws up his last will and testament to reflect only his desires concerning the disbursement of his estate, that is, without regard for the opinions and wishes of others, and just as those wishes are carried out following his death regardless of what anyone else may think about it, so Jesus Christ took the sole initiative for the terms of the new covenant.

The new covenant was not in effect until the work of the Cross. Just as a human will or testament does not take effect until the person making the will dies, so the new covenant awaited the death of Jesus to go into effect. Prior to the death of Jesus, then, the reigning covenant was still the one established with Israel at Sinai. Jesus Christ was born "under the law" (Galatians 4:4), while the law of Moses was still in effect. Though the law was waning in its influence and was soon to meet its demise, it was the covenant current from Mount Sinai to Mount Calvary.

For this reason, we must recognize a sharp distinction between the dealings of God with humanity prior to and after the Cross. The Cross ushered in a new era, characterized by the new covenant. The Hebrew prophets foretold several characteristics of the new covenant that were radically distinct from the old covenant: (1) It is unlike the old covenant, which was established with Israel at

Sinai (Jeremiah 31:32). (2) It involves an internal work in the hearts of people rather than simply making demands for external observance (Jeremiah 31:33). (3) It offers a superior knowledge of God (Jeremiah 31:34). (4) It includes forgiveness of sins (Jeremiah 31:34). (5) It involves the Holy Spirit coming upon believers (Isaiah 59:21; Ezekiel 36:26-27; Joel 2:28-29). (6) It results in an increased awe for God (Jeremiah 32:40). (7) It includes an atonement for sins (Ezekiel 16:60-63). (8) It provides justification (right standing with God) (Ezekiel 36:25). (9) It provides regeneration (the new birth) (Ezekiel 36:26). (10) It provides sanctification (a holy life) (Ezekiel 36:27).

When John the Baptist prepared the way for the Messiah, he declared that Jesus was the one who would baptize with the Holy Spirit (Mark 1:8; John 1:33). Jesus Himself declared that those who believe on Him would receive the Holy Spirit (John 7:37-39), but not until after His glorification, which, of course, followed His death. Just before His departure from this earth, following His death and resurrection, Jesus told His disciples, "For John truly baptized with water, but you shall be baptized with the Holy Spirit not many days from now" (Acts 1:5, NKJV). Jesus identified the baptism with the Holy Spirit as the promise of the Father (Acts 1:4; 2:33), meaning the promise of God recorded in the Old Testament to pour out His Spirit.

All the Old Testament promises concerning the coming of the Spirit, the prophecy of John the Baptist, and the promise made by Jesus began to be fulfilled on the Day of Pentecost, when the Holy Spirit came upon all of the gathered disciples, filling them and speaking through them in languages they had never learned (Acts 2:1-4). According to Peter, who possessed the keys of the kingdom (Matthew 16:19), this event fulfilled Joel's prophecy concerning the pouring out of God's Holy Spirit (Acts 2:16-18).

Thus the Day of Pentecost ushered in a new era, the era of the new covenant. From that day forward, as Jesus had predicted, all those who believed on Jesus received the Holy Spirit. (See Acts 8:15-17; 9:17; 10:44-46; 11:15-17; 15:7-9; 19:1-7; Romans 8:9, 11, 14-16; I Corinthians 12:13; Galatians 3:2-5; 5:16, 22-25; Ephesians 1:13; 3:16; 5:18; Hebrews 2:3-4; 6:4; Jude 20.) The death of Jesus Christ made this new era possible.

Verses 18-19. To prefigure that the shedding of Messiah's blood would establish the new covenant, the first covenant—the law of Moses—was also dedicated with blood. As an indication of the inferiority of the old covenant, the blood by which it was established was the blood of animals.

After Moses read the law to the people of Israel, he sprinkled the blood of calves and goats on the book itself and on the people. (See Exodus 24:3-8.) The blood sprinkled upon the book apparently indicated the activation of the covenant itself, and the blood sprinkled upon the people indicated their identification as the people upon whom the covenant was binding.

The Hebrew Scriptures themselves do not inform us about the use of "water, scarlet wool, and hyssop" (NKJV) in this ceremony or of the sprinkling of blood upon the book. This information was apparently preserved in Jewish tradition. The Exodus account reveals that Moses sprinkled blood upon the altar (representing God Himself as one of the parties to the covenant) and the people (representing the other party to the covenant).

Verse 20. After Moses had read the words of the covenant and sprinkled the blood, he said to the people of Israel, "This is the blood of the covenant which God has commanded you" (NKJV). The writer of Hebrews presented Moses' statement in somewhat different words from the Hebrew text: "This is the blood of the covenant which the Lord has made with you according to all these words" (Exodus 24:8, NKJV). The meaning in Hebrews is inherent in Moses' statement as recorded in Exodus. The phrase "which the Lord has made with you according to all these words" reflects the idea of "which God has commanded you." The old covenant was, after all, characterized by the Ten Commandments. It was a bilateral covenant that required for its performance the faithfulness of two parties: God and Israel. God could be counted on to keep His part of the covenant, and the people of Israel declared, "All that the LORD has said we will do, and be obedient" (Exodus 24:7, NKJV). They failed, of course, to live up to their commitment. (See Jeremiah 11:10.)

The statement of Moses at the inception of the old covenant bears remarkable resemblance to the statement of Jesus just prior to the inauguration of the new covenant. At the institution of the Lord's Supper, Jesus said, "For this is My blood of the new covenant, which is shed for many for the remission of sins" (Matthew 26:28, NKJV). This similarity would not have been lost on His disciples, all of whom were thoroughly acquainted with the words of Moses as recorded in the Torah. Though the disciples doubtless did not fully grasp the import of Jesus' words at the time, they did later as the awareness came to them that the death of Jesus was God's way of terminating one covenant and establishing another. Each celebration of the Lord's Supper brought this truth back to their attention, as Paul indicated: "In the same manner He also took the cup after supper, saying, 'This cup is the new covenant in My blood: this do, as often as you drink it, in remembrance of Me'" (I Corinthians 11:25, NKJV). Just as the Jewish Passover had constantly refocused the nation's vision on God's intervention in delivering them from Egyptian slavery, so the observance of the Lord's Supper constantly refocused the vision of the early church on the termination of the old covenant and the establishment of the new covenant in Christ's blood.

Verse 21. Not only did Moses inaugurate the law by the sprinkling of blood upon the people, the book, and the altar built at the foot of Mount Sinai; he also sprinkled with blood the Tabernacle and the sacred vessels upon their completion. The Hebrew Scriptures record the sprinkling of blood upon the altar, but not the sprinkling of the Tabernacle itself and of all the vessels (Exodus 29:12). Here the writer of Hebrews no doubt drew upon Jewish tradition, which preserved this information and was common knowledge to his original readers.[26] The Old Testament does not record everything that happened in each event to which it alludes; some of these things were preserved by oral tradition and written down much later in sources like Josephus, Philo, and the Talmud. Where this information is included by inspiration in the New Testament, we can be certain of its accuracy. This certainty does not extend to Jewish traditions not supported by the New Testament.

The sprinkling of the blood of animals on the Tabernacle (which was the dwelling place of God, Exodus 25:8) and its vessels demonstrated their identification with the old covenant itself. The Tabernacle was essential to the covenant; one could have no meaningful existence without the other. Similarly, under the new covenant, the church is the dwelling place of God (I Corinthians 3:16-17; II Corinthians 6:16); the church depends upon the new covenant for its meaning and existence.

Verse 22. Under the provisions of the law of Moses, "almost all things are purified with blood" (NKJV). The word "almost" retains a provision for the poor, who could not afford a blood sacrifice, to offer a substitute. (See Leviticus 5:11-13.) Even in this case, however, the flour offered was a substitute for blood. Thus, the writer of Hebrews could declare, "Without shedding of blood there is no remission" (NKJV).

Leviticus 17:11 explains why the blood was necessary: "For the life of the flesh is in the blood, and I have given it to you upon the altar to make atonement for your souls; for it is the blood that makes atonement for the soul" (NKJV). This identification of "life" with "blood" indicates a mutuality of value. Since "life" and "blood" are virtually identical, they become synonyms, and the value of one is equivalent to the value of the other. From this identification we see why the blood of Christ could atone for the sins of the whole world: Since He was not only man but also God, His blood—or His life—was of infinite value. The sacrifice of His life was of more value than the entirety of creation. (See Acts 20:28.) Leviticus 17:11 also points out that under the law, the blood atoned only as it was "upon the altar," that is, only in conjunction with the death of the sacrificial animal. To say, "Without shedding of blood there is no remission" is to say, "Without death there is no remission."

The blood shed under the law did not take away sin (10:4); it offered purification from ceremonial or ritual uncleanness. It was but a pale shadow of the blood of Christ, which, due to His identity as God, was efficacious in remitting sin. The word "remission," translated from the Greek *aphesis*, literally means "sending away." Essentially, the word "remission" is synonymous with "forgiveness."

Verse 23. Everything associated with the Tabernacle was a copy of heavenly things. (See comments on 8:2, 4-5.) This statement does not mean that in heaven there is a physical tent identical in appearance to the Tabernacle in the wilderness. The word translated "patterns" (KJV) and "copies" (NKJV) (Greek, *hypodeigmata*) means a "sample," "suggestion," "outline," "token," or "example."[27] What Moses saw in Exodus 25:9, 40 was not a physical tent in heaven, but a "pattern." The Tabernacle constructed under the law was thus the copy of a pattern, not the reproduction of a celestial Tabernacle already in existence.

Contextually, the heavenly reality of which the Tabernacle was merely a copy is "the presence of God" (verse 24). The earthly Tabernacle provided a place where God could meet with the Israelites (Exodus 25:8) through the obscurity of clouds of incense as they were represented by one man (the high priest) in the most remote and forbidden chamber (the Holy of Holies) on only one day out of the year. How different this was from the immediate and intimate access into the very presence of God that the blood of Jesus gained for all believers!

In heaven we will not see a Tabernacle like that of the law of Moses, sectioned off into increasingly taboo chambers, the most remote of which is accessible only to the few who happen to meet the stringent qualifications. Instead, like the apostle John, we will see "no temple in it, for the Lord God Almighty and the Lamb are its temple" (Revelation 21:22, NKJV). The word here translated "are" (Greek, *estin*) is actually the third person singular form of *eimi* ("to be"), meaning "is." Since it is singular, not plural, it draws together the Lord God Almighty and the Lamb into one entity. Subjects and verbs must agree in number; a singular verb demands a singular subject. When Revelation 22:1-4 speaks of God and the Lamb, it describes one throne, one face, and one name. It uses singular pronouns to refer to God and the Lamb ("his," "him"). The point is that the Lamb, Jesus Christ (John 1:29), is the visible manifestation of the invisible God Himself. (See I Timothy 3:16; John 1:14; Hebrews 1:3; Colossians 1:15.)

The "copies of the things in the heavens" (NKJV), that is, the Tabernacle built by the ancient Israelites and all of its furnishings and equipment, were purified by the sprinkling of the blood of animals. The plural "these" is apparently a reference to the plural sprinklings, first on the book, the altar and the people at the foot of Sinai (verse 19), then on the Tabernacle and all its vessels (verse 21). The word "purified" is translated from the Greek *katharizesthai*, which has to do with cleansing. Since the blood of animals could not eradicate moral impurity (10:4), this was a ceremonial or ritual cleansing which, like all the rituals of the law, were symbolic of a greater reality. (See comments on verse 9.)

The ritual cleansing of the earthly copies represented the future genuine cleansing of the "heavenly things" with "better sacrifices" than those of the law of Moses. At least nine views have been advanced as to what these "heavenly things" are. Since there can be no sin in heaven in need of cleansing (Revelation 21:27), the most satisfactory solution seems to be that the true Tabernacle refers to the sphere of communion between God and man. As MacLeod pointed out, "The sacrifice of Christ opened up a way of access to God's presence and keeps it open. As sinful pilgrims on their way to the heavenly city, God's people defile all they touch, even their 'meeting place' with God, and they need the constant efficacy of the sacrifice of Christ their high priest to remove that defilement."[28] Not only does the blood of Jesus gain access for us into the presence of God; it continually holds the door of access open as it perpetually cleanses us from sin (I John 1:7).

The cleansing of the earthly Tabernacle with blood was "necessary," because in God's economy "without shedding of blood there is no remission" (verse 22, NKJV). If the shedding of animal blood was necessary to provide ritual cleansing under the law, it was also necessary for "the heavenly things" to be cleansed with "better sacrifices." This is another way of saying that the sacrifices of the old covenant did not actually remit sins (10:4). They were symbols of the sacrifice that would.

That the heavenly things are cleansed with "better sacrifices" does not mean the one sacrifice of Christ is insufficient. In view of the author's insistence that Christ's singular sacrifice was sufficient (9:28; 10:10, 14), we should understand the word "sacrifices" as a generic plural that, still in the language of the old covenant, states the necessity of sacrifice to deal with the sin problem.[29] The focus is not on how many sacrifices are necessary under the new covenant, but on the need for something superior to the blood of animals to cleanse the heavenly things.

Verse 24. In contrast to the high priests under the law of Moses, Christ—as the great High Priest (4:14)—did not enter the holy places of the earthly Tabernacle. This point alone indicates the inferiority of all associated with the old covenant. The Tabernacle was not the ultimate dwelling place of God, which awaited the arrival of the great High Priest to enjoy its fullest glory; the Tabernacle's greatest glory was in the service of imperfect human priests. It would never rise above that. That Christ never entered the earthly holy places shows there was no need for Him to do so. The glory of the Holy Place and the Most Holy Place paled in comparison to the true Holiest of Holies, heaven itself. The holy places "made with hands" were merely "copies" (NKJV) or "figures" (KJV) of the true. (See comments on verse 23.)

What characterizes the true Holy Place is the presence of God. In contrast to the rare annual visit of the lone high priest to the Most Holy Place of the Tabernacle, where clouds of incense shrouded the presence of God, Christ has gained access on our behalf into the immediate and unmitigated presence of God. The word translated "presence" (Greek, *prosopon*) literally means "face," indicating the complete openness of communion, and "person," indicating the genuineness of the encounter.

By His own blood, the Messiah entered into the immediate presence of God Himself. This statement does not mean that Christ is someone other than God, but that He

49

has passed from the human and earthly realm into the heavenly realm. The human Messiah ("Christ") now resides in heaven itself on behalf of all human beings whose faith is in Him. His appearance there in the presence of God demonstrates with certainty that we will all one day stand with Him in that ultimate Holy Place. Just as under the law the high priest entered the Most Holy Place on behalf of all the people, so Christ has entered heaven on our behalf. But here again we see the inferiority of the law of Moses: the Aaronic high priest could never invite the people to join him in his annual pilgrimage into the Most Holy Place. But Jesus declared, "And if I go and prepare a place for you, I will come again and receive you to Myself; that where I am, there you may be also" (John 14:3, NKJV).

Verses 25-26. Since the one sacrifice of Jesus was of infinite value, it alone was sufficient to resolve once and for all the sin problem. (See verses 28; 10:10, 14.) Unlike the high priest who was required annually to make another sacrifice and to sprinkle its blood on the Day of Atonement to gain entrance into the Most Holy Place, Jesus appeared "once at the end of the ages . . . to put away sin by the sacrifice of Himself" (NKJV). Christ's sacrifice did not merely deal with sin temporarily: it "put away" sin. The word translated "put away" is a form of *aphesin*, frequently translated "remit" and "forgive." Here we see the finality of Christ's sacrifice. It was not necessary for Him to "suffer often since the foundation of the world" (NKJV). His blood was not a partial solution or a temporary solution; it was complete and final. This message would not have been lost on the original readers of this book who were being tempted to revert to Judaism. The inferiority of the law of Moses was evident by the necessity to offer sacrifices again and again. Obviously, no one sacrifice was sufficient. On the contrary, the death of Jesus so completely dealt with sin that no further sacrifice was necessary.

Verses 27-28. It is necessary that all human beings die once. It is not necessary for them to experience the "second death" (Revelation 20:14). Only those who have not experienced the second birth will experience the second death. As someone expressed it, "Be born once, die twice. Be born twice, die once." Adam's sin brought physical death on the entire human race (Genesis 3:19; Romans 5:12-14). To die physically is not to cease to exist or to lose consciousness. (See Luke 16:19-31.) It is merely the separation of the immaterial part of a person (spirit/soul) from the material part (body). (See Revelation 6:9-10.) The believer who dies is consciously and immediately in the presence of the Lord (II Corinthians 5:1-8; Philippians 1:23; Luke 23:43). The unbeliever who dies is consciously and immediately in a place of torment (Luke 16:19-24; II Peter 2:9).

Not only must all human beings die, they must—after death—face judgment. (See John 5:28; Acts 24:15.) For the believer, this is the judgment seat of Christ, which will occur after the bodies of the believers are resurrected in a glorified state and reunited with their soul/spirit. (See I Thessalonians 4:13-16; I Corinthians 15:22-23, 35-53; Philippians 3:21.) This is the first resurrection (Revelation 20:4-6). The judgment seat of Christ is not a judgment to determine salvation; only the saved will appear there. It is a judgment to determine rewards. (See Romans 14:10; I Corinthians 3:12-15; II Corinthians 5:10.)

The judgment unbelievers must face is the final judgment, sometimes called the Great White Throne Judgment. (See Revelation 20:11-15.) Although the Bible does not describe the resurrection body of unbelievers, we may be sure it will be suited to their fate, which is the lake of fire (Revelation 20:15).

The necessity of the singular death of human beings underscores that Christ was offered only once to bear the sins of many. Just as people must die only once, it was necessary for Him to be offered only once. The word "many" does not mean that by His death He bore the sins of many but not all. In this verbal allusion to Isaiah 53:12, the contrast is "between the one sacrifice and the great number of those who benefit from it."[30] In Hebrew thought, "the many" was a reference to the entire human race.

Verse 25 says Christ offered Himself. Here, we find the passive participle (Christ "was offered"). This construction no doubt arises since the author has in mind the great atonement passage of Isaiah 53, which describes the Messiah as being made an offering for sin (Isaiah 53:10).

Both here and in I Peter 2:24, the Bible says Christ bore the sins of the human race. He took the penalty of sin upon Himself.[31] This is also the meaning of II Corinthians 5:21. Since Jesus fully bore the penalty of sin Himself, there is no penalty left for human beings to bear, if they will put their trust in His work on their behalf.

Since Jesus dealt permanently with the sin problem on the cross, His second appearance to those who eagerly wait for Him will be "apart from sin, for salvation" (NKJV). This is not a reference to His sinlessness, which the book has well documented (4:15; 7:26-27), but it means that unlike His first appearance, His second will be without reference to sins.[32] Christ's second coming will be in reference to salvation, not sin. The ultimate outworking of the salvation provided by the blood of Jesus—final and utmost deliverance from sin and all its consequences—will occur at His second coming.

Christ's second appearance will be "to those who eagerly wait for Him" (NKJV). This statement harmonizes perfectly with the teaching of Paul concerning the Rapture of the church (I Thessalonians 4:13-18). It will be an appearance only to believers, not to the world at large. Paul three times used the same Greek word (*apekdechomenois*) that is here translated "eagerly wait" (NKJV), also in reference to the second appearance of Christ to believers. (See I Corinthians 1:7; Galatians 5:5; Philippians 3:20.)

I.

Christ's Sacrifice Is Superior to the Old Covenant Sacrifices (10:1-39)

1. The Law Was a Shadow (10:1-4)

(1) For the law having a shadow of good things to come, and not the very image of the things, can never with those sacrifices which they offered year by year continually make the comers thereunto perfect. (2) For then would they not have ceased to be offered? because that the worshippers once purged should have had no more conscience of sins. (3) But in those sacrifices there is a remembrance again made of sins every year. (4) For it is not possible that the blood of bulls and of goats should take away sins.

To this point, the writer of Hebrews has alluded to the inferiority and inadequacy of the sacrifices of the law of Moses (9:12-14, 23), but here he moved to a clear emphasis on the superiority of Christ's sacrifice. All of the sacrifices associated with the law were mere shadows in which God took no pleasure. They were unable to take away sins. What all those sacrifices from the construction of the Tabernacle in about 1400 B.C. to the destruction of the Temple in A.D. 70 could not accomplish even when added together, the death of Christ accomplished in a moment of time, once and for all.

This section of the book gives a strong warning to the original readers that there is nothing left in the old covenant—the law of Moses—to which to return. There was never any substance there anyway, and now even the shadow had been taken away. To abandon the new covenant in favor of a vanished shadow would be to sin willfully and to risk the vengeance of God. The section ends with an appeal not to "draw back to perdition," which would be the consequence of returning to the law, but to continue to "believe to the saving of the soul," which means continuing to have faith in Jesus Christ and His work on the cross.

Verse 1. Here, in a precise statement, we see the purpose and limitation of the law of Moses. God never intended the law to be an end in itself. In a statement similar to Paul's "the law was our tutor to bring us to Christ" (Galatians 3:24, NKJV), the writer of Hebrews declared that it had a mere "shadow of the good things to come" (NKJV), and that it was incapable of perfecting those who approached God on the basis of its sacrifices.

Contextually, the "good things to come" refer to the provisions of the new covenant in Christ Jesus. (See verses 10, 14, 16-23.) The law offered only a "shadow" (Greek, *skia*) of these things. *Skia* appears in 8:5 together with *hypodeigma* (see comments on verse 23) to describe the manner in which the ministry associated with the Aaronic priesthood was a "copy and shadow of the heavenly things" (NKJV). In Colossians 2:17, Paul used *skia* to categorize the dietary laws, the feast days, the new moons, and the sabbaths of the law as shadows "of things to come." In contrast to these shadows, the "substance is of Christ."

Since the law offered only a shadow, it did not possess "the very image of the things," or the good things to come, the provisions found only in Christ and the new covenant established in His blood. Nowhere in Scripture do we see more clearly that words are defined by their contexts. The word translated "image" (Greek, *eikon*) ordinarily indicates a representation of the real thing. Jesus used the word to refer to the physical likeness of Caesar on a coin (Matthew 22:20). Paul used it to describe idols shaped like human beings (Romans 1:23). John used *eikon* of the image of the beast, probably a physical likeness (Revelation 13:14-15). In another context, Paul used the word to describe the image of Adam in every person (I Corinthians 15:4-9). A total likeness is in view: body, soul, and spirit. In yet another context, he relied on *eikon* to express a likeness of quality or character, not a physical likeness. (See Romans 8:29; I Corinthians 11:7; II Corinthians 3:18; Colossians 3:10.) In I Corinthians 15:49, *eikon* again emphasizes quality or character, but also reaches out to embrace physical likeness.

Here, however, the word "image" refers to the reality itself in contrast to the shadow. This meaning is highly significant because some passages say Christ is the image of the invisible God (II Corinthians 4:4; Colossians 1:15). A physical likeness is not in view, because God is a Spirit and has no body, but what is in view is an exact representation of God in man. In other words, whatever God is, Jesus is. The *eikon* is so precise and complete that we can actually say that Jesus is God Himself.

The root word from which *eikon* comes is *eiko*, which

means "like," and it is used only in James 1:6, 23, first to compare a man with wavering faith to a wave of the sea and next a person who hears the word but does not do it to someone who looks in a mirror but does nothing about what it shows him.

The basic idea is that one thing or person is like another in some way. The word *eikon* seems to find its ultimate expression when used to describe how Jesus is like God. The likeness is so complete that there is no distinguishing between Jesus and God. He *is* God in flesh. To say that one is *like God* is not the same as saying one is like Caesar or any other use of *eikon*, for God is unique. "To whom then will ye liken me, or shall I be equal? saith the Holy One"(Isaiah 40:25). (See also Isaiah 40:18; 46:5.) For Jesus to be like Him, He must be Him, albeit in a visible manifestation. Since the image of God in Jesus is not a reference to a physical body, the likeness must be that of essence, and since the essence of deity is unique, there can be no difference between the deity that dwelt in Jesus and the nature of God before the Incarnation. Jesus as the image of God is God incarnate. The humanity itself was not God, but the deity was miraculously and mysteriously manifest in every aspect of the authentic humanness of Jesus.

Since *eikon* in Hebrews 10:1 refers to the reality, we can also say that the use of *eikon* to describe Jesus as the image of God also refers to the reality of His deity.

Since the law consisted of shadows and every sacrifice was merely a representation of something good to come, those sacrifices, though offered year after year, could never make perfect those who approached God by means of them. The word "perfect" (Greek, *teleiosai*) does not refer to sinless perfection. Verse 2 defines it as freedom from consciousness of sins. That is, since the sacrifices themselves were only shadows incapable of taking away sins (verse 4), they were not able to effect a clear conscience. Even after the high priest approached the Most Holy Place and executed the elaborate rituals of the Day of Atonement flawlessly, neither he nor the people of Israel had a sense of release from sin. Instead, they were simply reminded again that they were sinful people (verse 3).

Verse 2. We see the inability of the sacrifices of the law to deal with the sin problem in that they had to be offered again and again. If those sacrifices had been sufficient to remove sin, it would not have been necessary to repeat them. They did not purify the worshipers; those who offered the sacrifices were left with a lingering consciousness of sins.

Here, by implication, we see a marvelous consequence of the sacrifice of Christ. Since His sacrifice—in contrast to the sacrifices of the law—was efficacious, it purifies those who approach God through Christ Jesus and leaves them with no more consciousness of sins. Because His blood does remit sin, we can "draw near with a true heart in full assurance of faith, having our hearts sprinkled from an evil conscience" (verse 22, NKJV).

Also by implication we see here that the one sacrifice of Christ was sufficient. (See verses 10, 14 and 9:25-28.) When a sacrifice can perfect those who approach God on its basis, there is no need for any further sacrifice. At that point, sacrifices can cease. (See verse 18.)

Verse 3. The sacrifices associated with the law of Moses served as annual reminders of the sinfulness of the people. Since the word translated "reminder" (NKJV)

(Greek, *anamnesis*) appears in the New Testament only here and in the establishment of the Lord's Supper (Luke 22:19; I Corinthians 11:24-25), there is a strong implication of a connection between the two. Just as the sacrifices of the law continually reminded the people of Israel of their sinfulness, so the bread and cup of the Lord's Supper continually remind believers of the new covenant established in Christ's blood and of the cleansing from sin thereby provided.

Verse 4. The height of the sacrificial system under the law was the Day of Atonement, on which the high priest offered the blood of a bull for himself and his family and the blood of a goat for the people of Israel. (See comments on 9:7.) If these sacrifices were incapable of taking away sin, we may be sure all lesser sacrifices suffered the same limitation.

The word translated "take away" (Greek, *aphaireo*) is a strong one. It is used to describe the way Peter cut off the ear of the high priest's servant (Luke 22:50) and the way the conception took away reproach of Elizabeth's barrenness (Luke 1:25). The new covenant implication is that the offering of the body of Christ was able to do what the blood of bulls and goats could not do: The blood of Jesus took away sins as decisively as Peter's sword sliced off a man's ear and as Elizabeth's conception eradicated her reproach.

2. The Messiah's Confession
(10:5-9)

(5) Wherefore when he cometh into the world, he saith, Sacrifice and offering thou wouldest not, but a

body hast thou prepared me: (6) in burnt offerings and sacrifices for sin thou hast had no pleasure. (7) Then said I, Lo, I come (in the volume of the book it is written of me,) to do thy will, O God. (8) Above when he said, Sacrifice and offering and burnt offerings and offering for sin thou wouldest not, neither hadst pleasure therein; which are offered by the law; (9) then said he, Lo, I come to do thy will, O God. He taketh away the first, that he may establish the second.

Verses 5-7. Here the writer of Hebrews offered a form of the Septuagint version of Psalm 40:6-8, which is itself "an interpretative paraphrase of the Hebrew text."[33] The Book of Hebrews frequently appeals to the Septuagint, or a form of it. (See comments on 1:6, 10-12; 2:5, 12-13, 17; 3:7-11.) There is no problem here concerning the integrity of Scripture; the writer of Hebrews was inspired of God in his use of the Septuagint or any variation of it. For this reason, the context relevant to understanding this quote is the immediate context here in Hebrews, not the context of Psalm 40:6-8. Not all of Psalm 40 in its original context is Messianic, for verse 12 says, "My iniquities have overtaken me, so that I am not able to look up" (NKJV), and the Messiah had no sin. But here, as elsewhere, God inspired the writer of Hebrews to use portions of Old Testament passages and to invest new or additional meaning in them pertaining to the Messiah.

This passage is incarnational. It has to do with what the Messiah said to God in conjunction with His entrance into the world. It is not a communication between persons in the Godhead, nor does it apply prior to the Incarnation. The word translated "cometh" in the KJV (Greek, *eiserchomenos*) is a present tense participle that functions in the active voice. The KJV translation of this word ("cometh") is more precise than that of the NKJV ("came"). The idea in *eiserchomenos* is "coming." The verb *legei* is translated "he saith" by the KJV, which again is more accurate than the "He said" of the NKJV. *Legei* is the third person singular present active indicative form of *lego* and means "he says" or "he is saying." This is the idea in the old English "saith."

When did the Messiah make this statement? The KJV reads, "When he cometh into the world, he saith . . ." In today's English, this means, "When he is coming into the world, he is saying . . ." The tenses suggest that the Messiah made this statement shortly after the assumption of His human nature, perhaps at His birth, since the phrase "coming into the world" is a Jewish expression for birth.[34]

But this conclusion is problematic in view of the questions concerning the development of the Messiah's human consciousness. If He experienced human existence as do all other human beings—and that is what Scripture declares—then His human consciousness developed. (See Luke 2:52.) Thus, the Messiah did not have a fully aware human consciousness at birth to enable Him to make a statement like this.

Actually, the word "when" does not appear in the Greek text of verse 5, and this fact may help resolve the question. The verse itself does not indicate precisely when the Messiah made this statement. The present participle "coming" (Greek, *eiserchomenos*) does indicate it could not have been prior to the Incarnation, as does the present active "He says" (Greek, *legei*). But since *legei* can be a "timeless present"[35] and the word "when" is absent, we may conclude simply that the Messiah made this statement at some point after the Incarnation. A literal translation would be, "Therefore, coming (or entering) the world, He says . . ." The statement "a body hast thou prepared me" indicates strongly that the entire quote comes after the Incarnation. The word *katertiso*, translated "hast thou prepared" by the KJV, is in the aorist tense, which means it was accomplished in the past. Since the body was already prepared, and since this statement was made in conjunction with the Incarnation, the Messiah could have said it at any time during His life on earth prior to His crucifixion.

We should understand this communication between the Messiah and God in the same sense as all the prayers of Jesus. (See comments on 5:7.) It is not a conversation between two divine persons, but a genuinely human Messiah communicating with God from His human psyche, which He possessed as surely as a human body (verse 5), and whose mission was to do the will of God (verse 7). In the mystery of the Incarnation, the Messiah was, of course, the brightness of God's glory and the express image of God's person. (See comments on 1:3.) But His deity did not obscure or overwhelm His humanity; the Incarnation manifested God in human existence. (See John 1:14.) The Incarnation, the greatest of miracles, is a mystery, as are all miracles. (See I Timothy 3:16.) Scripture states the truth of the Incarnation but does not tell us precisely how the Incarnation worked. We must confess all that the Scripture says to be true, both as to Christ's deity and humanity, but we cannot offer a complete explanation without clouding or confusing either the deity or the humanity of Christ. It is enough to say that Jesus was both God and man.

The Incarnation involved God emptying Himself. (See Philippians 2:7, where the Greek *heauton ekenosen,* translated "made himself of no reputation" by the KJV, more properly means "emptied Himself.") He did so not by giving up any of His deity, but by "taking the form of a bondservant, and coming in the likeness of men" (NKJV). Thus we must confess that Jesus is the "human face of God." In the Incarnation Jesus did not consider the appearance of divine essence something to be retained (Philippians 2:6);[36] instead, His humanity was so genuine and complete that He experienced everything common to humans, including the need to pray and commune with God. How He could *be* God and yet pray is an enigma, but it is one we must accept.

To attempt the resolve this tension by suggesting that Jesus is a second person in the Godhead praying to the first person solves nothing but creates new problems. It does not explain why one divine person would need to pray to another or how such prayers could be valid. It does not explain how one divine person could honestly say to another, "Not My will, but Yours, be done" (Luke 22:42, NKJV). If the radical monotheism of Scripture (see Deuteronomy 6:4) permits the one God to exist as two or three distinct but completely equal persons, how could one confess to have a different desire or will from another? For that matter, as in our present context, how could one say to another, "I have come . . . to do Your will, O God"? (verse 7).

The best way to think about the conversations between the Messiah and God is to attribute them to the genuineness and fullness of Christ's human existence. He was a man, so He shared fully in the experiences of man, including the need for prayer.

The word "wherefore" or "therefore" (NKJV) refers back to the immediately preceding verses, which discuss the inability of the levitical sacrifices to take away sins. The Messiah's ministry was the divinely ordained response to the inadequacy of the law of Moses in dealing with sin.

The Messiah's incarnational confession, as translated by the NKJV, was, "Sacrifice and offering You did not desire, but a body You have prepared for Me. In burnt offerings and sacrifices for sin You had no pleasure. Then I said, 'Behold, I have come—in the volume of the book it is written of Me—to do Your will, O God.'"

The sacrifices, offerings, burnt offerings and sacrifices for sin are those "offered according to the law" (verse 8, NKJV). That is, the reference here is not to abuses of the sacrificial system of the law of Moses, but to the sacrificial system itself as found in the law. This verse thus indicates the temporary nature of the law. From its inception, the law was not something pleasing to God; He took no pleasure in the slaughter of animals, though this was the central event around which all the law revolved and which, in a sense, represented the law in its totality.

Why would God give to ancient Israel a covenant in which He took no pleasure? Paul addressed this question directly in Galatians 3:19-25: "What purpose then does the law serve? It was added because of transgressions. . . . The Scripture [the law] has confined all under sin. . . . We were kept under guard by the law. . . . The law was our tutor to bring us to Christ. . . . But after faith has come, we are no longer under a tutor" (NKJV).

We should probably understand the Greek *charin*, translated "because of," to refer to the goal, as it is in Titus 1:5, 11 and Jude 16—in this case, the goal of the law. That is, God gave the law to bring about transgressions.[37] The law was not merely a response to transgressions, for where there is no law, there is no transgression (Romans 4:15). This interpretation agrees with Romans 7:13: "Has then what is good become death to me? Certainly not! But sin, that it might appear sin, was producing death in me through what is good, so that sin through the commandment might become exceedingly sinful" (NKJV). Contextually, the reference to "what is good" is to the law. The point is that the law, in and of itself, does not separate people from God, but the sin nature in all human beings takes advantage of the law to produce even more sin and thus to separate people from fellowship with God. Here we see one of the major purposes of the law: it pointed out the sinfulness of humans and their inability to please God by their own strength.

God did not give Israel the law because it was His ultimate plan for redemption or because something inherent in the sacrificial system pleased Him. He gave Israel the law to demonstrate clearly to them the sinfulness of human nature, their inability to redeem themselves, and their desperate need of a Savior. This is the meaning of the statement, "The law was our tutor to bring us to Christ, that we might be justified by faith" (Galatians 3:24, NKJV). (See comments on verse 3.)

The words "sacrifice," "offering," "burnt offerings" and "sacrifices for sin" probably encompass the entire sacrificial system of the law. "Sacrifice" (Hebrew, *zebach*) could refer to the offering of any animal, but the Hebrew Scriptures use it to refer to the peace offering. "Offering" (Hebrew, *minchah*) as it pertains to the law specifically means the meal or cereal offering. The "burnt offering" (Hebrew, *'olah*) was an act of worship. The "sacrifices for sin" (Hebrew, *chatta'ah*) were for atonement.[38] The point is that what the entire scope of sacrifices under the law could not do, the one sacrifice of the body of the Messiah accomplished. (See also verse 10.)

The Hebrew text of Psalm 40:6 reads, "My ears you have opened," where the Septuagint has, "A body You have prepared for Me" (NKJV). The Septuagint is an interpretive rendering, understanding the ears to be representative of the entire body. Literally, the Hebrew reads, "My ears you have digged." This seems to refer to the creation of the human body, made from the earth (Genesis 2:7), in which the various orifices, including the ears, were "digged out." If the Messiah had a body, He would have ears. But it suits the purpose of the writer of Hebrews to quote the Septuagint, for his emphasis is on the body of the Messiah as the sacrifice that did what the sacrifices of the law could not do.

The Messiah came to do the will of God, which, in this context, was to take away the first covenant with its ineffectual sacrifices and to replace it with the new covenant by means of "the offering of the body of Jesus Christ once for all" (verses 9-10, NKJV).

The phrase "in the volume of the book it is written of Me" (NKJV) indicates the Christ-centered nature of the Pentateuch or Torah, the first five books of the Bible. The law of Moses, found in these books, existed to proclaim the good news of the coming Messiah; in direct statements and shadows, the law wrote of Him. This was

Jesus' point when He said to the unbelieving Jews, "You search the Scriptures, for in them you think you have eternal life; and these are they which testify of me" (John 5:39, NKJV). The Pharisees thought they could find eternal life in the study of the Scriptures alone; they did not understand that the very Scriptures they studied spoke of Jesus. To the disciples on the road to Emmaus, Jesus began "at Moses and all the Prophets" and "expounded to them in all the Scriptures the things concerning Himself" (Luke 24:27, NKJV). Later, to the larger apostolic circle, Jesus said, "These are the words which I spoke to you while I was still with you, that all things must be fulfilled which were written in the Law of Moses and the Prophets and the Psalms concerning Me" (Luke 24:44, NKJV).

Verses 8-9. Here the writer of Hebrews reiterated a portion of the previous verses, clarifying that the sacrifices, offerings, burnt offerings and offerings for sin he had in view were those "which are offered according to the law" (NKJV). Thus the problem with the sacrifices was not the attitude of those who offered them or the spiritual condition of Israel at large. In other words, the reason God did not desire these sacrifices or take pleasure in them was not because of lack of devotion or faith on the part of those offering the sacrifices. The sacrifices were offered according to the law, but they still brought Him no pleasure. They could not, for they were incapable of taking away sins under the best of conditions. (See verses 4, 11.) God could not be satisfied with a mere shadow. (See verse 1.)

Then, in a dramatic statement that should answer forever the relationship of the old covenant to the new covenant, verse 9 declares, "He takes away the first that He may establish the second" (NKJV). The "first" is the old covenant with its inadequate sacrificial system; the "second" is the new covenant with its efficacious offering. Here we clearly see that the two covenants cannot coexist. The new covenant is not merely an updated or revised or enhanced version of the old covenant. For the new covenant to be in effect, the old covenant had to be taken away. There is no compatibility between these covenants. One is a shadow; the other is the reality. (See comments on 8:6-13.)

3. The Finality of the Cross
(10:10-18)

(10) By the which will we are sanctified through the offering of the body of Jesus Christ once for all. (11) And every priest standeth daily ministering and offering oftentimes the same sacrifices, which can never take away sins: (12) but this man, after he had offered one sacrifice for sins for ever, sat down on the right hand of God; (13) from henceforth expecting till his enemies be made his footstool. (14) For by one offering he hath perfected for ever them that are sanctified. (15) Whereof the Holy Ghost also is a witness to us: for after that he had said before, (16) This is the covenant that I will make with them after those days, saith the Lord, I will put my laws into their hearts, and in their minds will I write them; (17) and their sins and iniquities will I remember no more. (18) Now where remission of these is, there is no more offering for sin.

Verse 10. The will of God, which the Messiah came to do (verse 7), was to provide sanctification once for all "through the offering of the body of Jesus Christ." The Greek word translated "sanctified" is derived from *hagios*, commonly related to holiness, separation and saints in the New Testament. The Hebrew idea of holiness is primarily separation unto something or someone and then by extension from something or someone. This verse describes the instantaneous positional sanctification or setting apart of believers unto God that occurs at regeneration. (See also I Corinthians 1:2; 6:11.) Verse 14 describes the progressive growth in practical sanctification that occurs as the believer daily seeks greater conformity to the character of Christ. (See also I Thessalonians 4:4.)

We should not think that the sacrifice of Jesus Christ on the cross involved only His physical body. In Hebrew thought, man is integrated so completely that to speak of one part of his existence is to speak of the whole. (See comments on 4:12.) In Isaiah 53:10, the "soul" of the Messiah is an offering for sin. As represented by His body, the entire human existence of the Messiah was involved in the Atonement. Since this is true, humans are completely redeemed. If only the body of the Messiah had been involved in redemption, presumably only the bodies of people would have been redeemed. But since the Fall in the Garden of Eden resulted in the corruption of not only the material but also the immaterial component of human existence, it was necessary that the Messiah's material and immaterial existence be involved in the redemptive act. His suffering was not limited to His physical body; it extended to His soul and spirit.

The sanctification provided by the Atonement was "once for all." There will never be a need for another sacrifice to complement that of Jesus Christ. He finished the work of redemption. (See John 19:30.) All that remains now is for humanity to appropriate His finished work through faith.

Verse 11 reiterates that the sacrifices offered according to the law could never take away sins. (See comments on verses 1, 4.) The statements in this verse are in the present tense (i.e., the priest "stands ministering daily . . . offering repeatedly the same sacrifices, which can never take away sins," NKJV), indicating that these activities were occurring even as this book was written. The same indication appears in verses 1, 3, 8. The implication is that the Book of Hebrews was written before the destruction of the Temple in A.D. 70. The presence of the Temple and its continuing sacrificial ritual intensified the temptation of the original readers of this book to return to the old covenant.

It is significant that the priests stood to offer the repeated daily sacrifices. Under the law of Moses, the priests could not offer sacrifices from a seated position. In contrast, Jesus Christ, after offering the only efficacious sacrifice, sat down (verse 12), indicating the finality of His sacrifice.

As in verse 4, the implication here is that what the sacrifices of the law could not do ("take away sins"), the offering of the body of Jesus did. (See comments on verse 4.)

Verse 12. The sacrifice of Jesus was "for sins." These words reveal the error of every theory of the Atonement that sees the death of Jesus as accomplishing anything less than or other than the actual removal of sins. In the blood of Jesus, sins are remitted (verse 18), so that God is justified in forgetting them (verse 17).

Throughout church history, a number of Atonement theories have been suggested, many of which seem to offer some valid insight while at the same time suffering limitations. Unlike the case with many doctrines, no church council has ever been held on this subject, and the discussion continues to this day.[39]

The development of any biblical doctrine must first take into account related doctrines. In the case of the Atonement, the broadest of these is the doctrine of God, since He is the offended party and also the One who must offer forgiveness, if any is to be offered.

Scripture presents God as being absolutely holy and sinless. By virtue of His very nature, He cannot countenance sin.

The law of God is not something impersonal, as suggested by some theories of the Atonement. It is rather an expression of God Himself. When humans disobeyed it, they disobeyed God, for God is the One who gave the law. Disobedience of God's law carried the death penalty (Genesis 2:15-17; Ezekiel 18:20; Romans 6:23).

Sinful humans are unable to do anything to help themselves, for no one is righteous, no one understands, and no one seeks after God in and of himself (Romans 3:10-11). Therefore, if there was to be an atonement, someone else had to make it on behalf of humans. The only one who could make such an atonement would be one who, while human, was not merely human. Only God could offer a sufficient price, since a sacrifice of infinite value would have to be made to atone for a world of sin.

In the person of Christ, God added humanity to His

deity in order to atone for the sins of humans. Since Jesus was a man who never sinned, He could die in place of people who had; since He was God His life was of infinite value.

The Hebrew word translated "atonement" (*kaphar*) means "to cover." In the Old Testament, sinners offered a sacrifice as a substitute for themselves, providing a covering for their sin by interposing a sacrifice between the sin and God.

The sacrificial animal had to be perfect in every way. The one who needed atonement presented the sacrificial animal to the priest and laid his hands upon it as a confession of guilt and as a symbolic transfer of that guilt to the animal (Leviticus 1:3-4).

The great atonement passage in the Old Testament is Isaiah 53. It pictures the coming Messiah, the suffering servant, as bearing the sins of the people (Isaiah 53:4-6).

Jesus cited Isaiah 53:12 as applying to His personal ministry (Luke 22:37). His primary purpose for coming into this world was the death of the cross (Mark 8:31). Jesus declared His death was a ransom, without specifying to whom it was paid (Matthew 20:28). He was a substitute, taking the place of others in death (John 15:13).

John the Baptist declared the substitutionary and sacrificial roles of the Messiah (John 1:29).

Even Caiaphas, the unbelieving high priest, was apparently an instrument in the hands of the sovereign God in declaring the substitutionary work of Christ (John 11:49-50; 18:14).

Under divine inspiration, the apostle Paul emphasized the wrath of God upon sin (Romans 1:18) and described the death of Christ as propitiatory. That is, it actually appeased the wrath of God against sin (Romans 3:25-26). Moreover, the Atonement was the work of God Himself in Christ (II Corinthians 5:19). It was a demonstration of the love of God (Romans 5:8). It was such a supreme price that it guaranteed all lesser gifts (Romans 8:32). Christ's death was a substitution (II Corinthians 5:14). Christ was the Passover lamb offered as a sacrifice (I Corinthians 5:7). Paul's many references to the blood of Christ clearly reveal the sacrificial nature of the Atonement (Romans 3:25; 5:9; Ephesians 1:7; 2:13; Colossians 1:20). Christ was made a curse for us (Galatians 3:13), and He died for us (I Thessalonians 5:10).

In summary, in the death of Christ God provided a sacrifice, fulfilling the Old Testament sacrificial system, to atone for the sins of humanity. This sacrifice was not merely a substitute; Christ actually bore in His body the sins of the world.

By the Atonement, God was propitiated (His just wrath against sin was satisfied) and He was thereby able to be merciful to sinful humans. Christ's death became the means of reconciliation between God and humanity, removing the barrier that hindered such a relationship.

While many of the Atonement theories that have been offered lack vital elements, there is some accuracy in many of them. It is true, for example, that the death of Christ gave us a perfect example of the dedication we should have toward God. It is true that the death of Christ demonstrated the boundless love of God for His creation. At the same time, it revealed the seriousness of sin and the certainty and severity of the judgment of a righteous God. The death of Christ was a victory over Satan and his evil forces, which liberated sinners from the grasp of the enemy. And the death of Christ rendered satisfaction to God for the sins of humanity.

But the death of Christ was much more than all of this. At the cross of Calvary, God took on Himself the sins of the human race, paying the penalty for sin, which was totally beyond the capability and reach of humanity. When Jesus Christ came forth from the tomb, He came as a conqueror over Satan and sin. Nothing remains to stand in the way of salvation for those who will have faith in the finished work of Calvary.

The Atonement includes both objective and subjective elements. Objectively, it satisfies God's righteous judgment and enables Him to turn in mercy to sinful humanity. Subjectively, it provides the basis for the grace of God to draw individuals to Christ.

Since the death of Christ was effective in removing sins, there is no need for any further offering (verse 18). That Jesus "sat down at the right hand of God" indicates that His redemptive work is finished. Priests must stand to offer their daily sacrifices, but Christ's seated position illustrates the finality of His work. (See comments on verse 11.)

For a discussion of "the right hand of God," see comments on 1:3 and 8:1.

Verse 13. From the time that Jesus finished His atoning work and sat down at the right hand of God, He has been waiting for His enemies to be subjugated to Him. (See comments on 1:3; 2:6-8.) Here we see the fulfillment of Psalm 110:1, to which the writer of Hebrews alluded earlier (1:13).

The enemies of Christ certainly include Satan and all who identify with him. Satan will be finally vanquished

75

when he is cast into the lake of fire (Revelation 20:10). This is also the fate of those whose names are not written in the Book of Life (Revelation 20:12-15). Perhaps the writer intended this comment as a warning to those who contemplated turning away from faith in the one offering of the body of Christ to return to the ineffective offerings of the law. (See verses 26-39.) If some did so, they would identify themselves as the enemies of God and thus could expect to suffer the fate reserved for all who oppose Him. The only way to avoid this destiny would be to hold the beginning of their confidence steadfast to the end (3:14).

Verse 14. Again Hebrews declares the finality of Christ's sacrifice. (See 9:25-28; 10:10, 12.) Since the offering of His body was efficacious, there was no need for any further offering. (See verse 18.) Christ's cross dealt with sin decisively and permanently. Nothing else needs to be done, and nothing else can be done to contribute to a resolution of the sin problem, either collectively or individually.

The context defines the perfection accomplished for people of faith by the Atonement as purification from sin, which includes the cleansing of the conscience from sins. (See verses 1-2.) It is not a reference to sinless perfection, or to the eradication of the sin nature, but to the forgiveness of sin extended to those who appropriate the provisions of the Cross. (See verse 18.) Those who are so forgiven, when they understand the completeness and finality of Christ's work, have no more consciousness of sins. (See verse 2.) That is, as opposed to the Israelites who were reminded of their sins every year on the Day of Atonement (verse 3), those who are cleansed by the blood of Christ need take no further thought of the sins so purged. Their sins are not merely covered; they are actually gone. (See comments on verses 4, 11.)

The perfection resulting from the provisions of the Atonement is permanent ("for ever"). A person who has through faith appropriated the provisions of the Cross will never need to do anything further to contribute to the purging of his sins.

Permanent perfection does not mean that if a person loses faith in Christ he retains his salvation, for the letter to the Hebrews warns of the dangers of losing faith in Christ and thus losing salvation. (See comments on 2:1-3; 3:12-14; 4:1, 4-6; 10:26-38.) Rather, the condition by which we appropriate the provisions of the Atonement—namely, faith in Christ—is the condition by which we retain them. Those who have "received the knowledge of the truth," which the larger context of the letter defines as the new covenant, but who "sin willfully" by turning away from the Son of God (verse 26), discounting the value of His blood and insulting the Spirit of grace (verse 29), will surely experience the vengeance of God (verse 30). They have cast away their confidence in Christ (verse 35) by drawing back from Christ and the new covenant to perdition (verse 39). Only those who continue to believe will be saved (verse 39).

The Greek *hagiazomenous* is translated "are sanctified" by the KJV, which one could interpret to mean a once-for-all event. But the word is a present passive participle, and the NKJV translates it more precisely as "are being sanctified."

It is true that, as verse 10 states, "we have been sanctified through the offering of the body of Jesus Christ once for all" (NKJV). That verse refers to positional or forensic

77

(legal) sanctification. We have been set apart unto God once for all by the sacrifice of Jesus Christ. There is nothing we can do to enhance that sanctification; there is nothing more effective than the blood of Jesus in separating us unto God.

But verse 14 apparently refers to the ongoing outworking of this sanctification in the believer's life. This verse has to do with progressive sanctification, the day-by-day growth in conformity to the character of Christ that every believer should experience. (See Romans 8:29; II Peter 3:18.) Believers have already been "perfected," or purified from their sins (verse 1), but they now need to bring their experiential Christianity into conformity with their positional Christianity. In this sense, the Christian life is the process of "becoming what we are." God does not wait until we bring every area of our lives into conformity with His character before He saves us, but He saves us to bring every area of our lives into conformity with His character. (See Ephesians 2:8-10.)

That *hagiazomenous* is in the passive voice indicates that this sanctification is not something the believer accomplishes by his own efforts. It is not merely the product of self-discipline. Rather, it is something accomplished in him by the "one offering" by which he is forever perfected. Philippians 2:12-13 describes this process well: "Work out your own salvation with fear and trembling; for it is God who works in you both to will and to do for His good pleasure" (NKJV). Though believers are to "work out" their own salvation, they do so as they respond to God's initiative in giving them the desire ("to will") and the ability ("to do") to perform His pleasure. Human works that represent an effort to earn God's favor are worthless (Romans 4:4-5; 11:6; Ephesians 2:8-9). But works that result from genuine faith responding to divine initiative contribute to the maturing of godly character in the believer. (See James 2:14-26; Hebrews 11.)

Verses 15-17 constitute an internal witness to the inspiration of Scripture. The writer of Hebrews agreed with Jesus, Peter, and Paul that the Scriptures were given by the Holy Spirit. (See Mark 12:36; Acts 1:16; 28:25; II Timothy 3:16; II Peter 1:21.) Scripture itself claims to have been given by the Holy Spirit, and we must either accept or reject that claim. If we accept it, we must acknowledge the supernatural origin of the Scriptures and thus their authority. If we reject it, only two options remain. Either the Scriptures were written by people who thought they were being moved by the Holy Spirit but who were not, in which case the Scriptures were written by deluded and thus mentally unstable people, or they were written by people who claimed to be moved by the Holy Spirit but who knew they were not. In this case, the Scriptures were written by liars.

But the nature of the Scriptures excludes the possibility that they were written by deluded or deceitful people. People who are mentally unstable do not write literature with the grand and consistent sweep of the Book that has been confessed to be the greatest literature in the world even by those who reject its supernatural origin. If these people were deluded, their efforts would have descended into senseless gibbering. Nor could or would liars have written a book like the Bible. Liars do not lift up the high moral tone of Scripture, which itself forbids lying. If the Bible had been written by deceitful people, their deceit would at some point have turned to self-serving ambition;

they would have written something to further their own carnal purposes. But nowhere in Scripture do we find evidence of such an attempt.

In the final analysis, the only reasonable decision is to agree with the witness of Scripture that it is of supernatural origin; it is given by the Holy Spirit.

Significantly, the word "witnesses" (NKJV) is in the present tense. Although the Scripture does consist of words written on paper or some other surface, it is a living witness, not a dead one. It did not merely speak in the past; it continues to speak. As Stephen testified, the Scriptures are "living oracles" (Acts 7:38, NKJV). Because of they originate with the eternal God, the words are just as potent and effective today as they were the first day they were spoken. In a sense, it is just as if God is continually speaking them to every generation.

The witness of the Holy Spirit to which the writer of Hebrews referred was the promise of the new covenant found in Jeremiah 31:33-34. He previously referred to this promise in 8:8-12 (see comments). In this case he collapsed the longer promise into a shorter statement: After promising to make a new covenant characterized by an inner work as opposed to the external nature of the law of Moses, the Holy Spirit added that He would no longer remember the sins and lawless deeds of the people.

This passage identifies the Holy Spirit with God Himself. It is the Holy Spirit who speaks (verse 15), who is the Lord (verse 16), and who further adds the words of verse 17. In its original context, Jehovah spoke this prophecy. Its attribution to the Holy Spirit here is as significant as the equation of the Holy Spirit with God in Acts 5:3-4. The Holy Spirit is God.

Verse 18. The offering of the body of Jesus Christ (verse 10) resulted in the remission of sins. (See Matthew 26:28.) The word "remission" is translated from *aphesis*, which is often translated "forgiveness." (See Mark 3:29; Acts 5:31; 13:38; 26:18; Ephesians 1:7; Colossians 1:14.) The essential meaning of *aphesis* is to "send away."

What the blood of bulls and goats was unable to do (verses 4, 11), the blood of Jesus did. Since the blood of Jesus was efficacious in removing sin, there is "no longer an offering for sin" (NKJV). That is, since the Atonement dealt completely and permanently with sin, no further offering needs to be made. The sacrifice of Jesus has made every other sacrifice for sin obsolete (8:13). On the basis of the offering of the body of Jesus Christ, God chooses to "remember no more" the sins and lawless deeds of those who put their trust in Him (verse 17). Jesus Christ has completely satisfied the penalty for sin.

4. Don't Draw Back from Christ
(10:19-39)

(19) Having therefore, brethren, boldness to enter into the holiest by the blood of Jesus, (20) by a new and living way, which he hath consecrated for us, through the veil, that is to say, his flesh; (21) and having an high priest over the house of God; (22) let us draw near with a true heart in full assurance of faith, having our hearts sprinkled from an evil conscience, and our bodies washed with pure water. (23) Let us hold fast the profession of our faith without wavering; (for he is faithful that promised;) (24) and

let us consider one another to provoke unto love and to good works: (25) not forsaking the assembling of ourselves together, as the manner of some is; but exhorting one another: and so much the more, as ye see the day approaching. (26) For if we sin wilfully after that we have received the knowledge of the truth, there remaineth no more sacrifice for sins, (27) but a certain fearful looking for of judgment and fiery indignation, which shall devour the adversaries. (28) He that despised Moses' law died without mercy under two or three witnesses: (29) of how much sorer punishment, suppose ye, shall he be thought worthy, who hath trodden under foot the Son of God, and hath counted the blood of the covenant, wherewith he was sanctified, an unholy thing, and hath done despite unto the Spirit of grace? (30) For we know him that hath said, Vengeance belongeth unto me, I will recompense, saith the Lord. And again, The Lord shall judge his people. (31) It is a fearful thing to fall into the hands of the living God. (32) But call to remembrance the former days, in which, after ye were illuminated, ye endured a great fight of afflictions; (33) partly, whilst ye were made a gazingstock both by reproaches and afflictions; and partly, whilst ye became companions of them that were so used. (34) For ye had compassion of me in my bonds, and took joyfully the spoiling of your goods, knowing in yourselves that ye have in heaven a better and an enduring substance. (35) Cast not away therefore your confidence, which hath great recompence of reward. (36) For ye have need of patience, that, after ye have done the will of God, ye might receive the promise. (37) For yet a little while, and he that shall come will come, and will not tarry. (38) Now the just shall live by faith: but if any man draw back, my soul shall have no pleasure in him. (39) But we are not of them who draw back unto perdition; but of them that believe to the saving of the soul.

Verse 19. Because we have in Christ a High Priest who is seated at the right hand of the throne of the Majesty in the heavens (8:1), and because He is a High Priest who has completely satisfied the righteous judgment of God upon sin by the offering of His body (verses 10-18), we can boldly enter the true Holiest Place by His blood. The word "therefore" refers back to the discussion of the atoning work of Christ and reveals its logical effect. The death of Christ on the cross did nothing less than to cleanse people of faith from their sins (verse 22) and to qualify them to enter directly into the presence of God.

The term "high priest" appears fifteen times in the Book of Hebrews, four times referring to high priests under the law of Moses (8:3; 9:7, 25; 13:11) and eleven times referring to Jesus Christ, the great High Priest (2:17; 3:1; 4:14, 15; 5:5, 10; 6:20; 7:26; 8:1; 9:11; 10:21). The teaching concerning Jesus Christ as the great high priest is the "solid food" (5:12, 14, NKJV) that is the main theme in this letter (8:1). (See discussion on 5:10-11.) That the final mention of Jesus Christ as High Priest appears in 10:21 indicates that this passage sums up all that Hebrews has previously said about Him in this capacity, including His atoning work. An understanding of the full effect of the blood of Jesus gives believers boldness to enter into the presence of God on the basis of that blood.

Where there is timidity in approaching God, there is a failure to appreciate fully the finality and completeness of the work of the Cross.

It is significant that the writer of Hebrews here referred to the original readers as "brethren." His previous uses of the word indicate a purposeful attempt to remind the original readers of the intimate relationship they have with the Messiah and with one another under the terms of the new covenant. (See comments on 2:11-12, 17; 3:1, 12.) His final use of the word also suggests an appeal to intimacy (13:22). This closeness contrasts to the distance from God that the rituals of the law of Moses forced upon the people of Israel. (See 12:18-21 and comments on 7:19.) Appealing to his readers as brethren seems to be a way of reminding them of the superiority of the new covenant.

This is not the first time that the Book of Hebrews mentions the boldness with which Christ's high priestly work enables us to enter God's presence. (See comments on 4:16.) Here, it says we have this boldness "to enter into the Holiest." Again we see that the Most Holy Place under the law of Moses symbolized the very presence of God Himself. (See comments on 9:3-5, 7-9.) In 4:14-16, the high priestly work of Christ gains the believer bold entry to the "throne of grace." Like the reference to the throne in 8:1, this phrase is simply a figure of speech for the presence of the God who is characterized by grace. When Hebrews says that Christ has not entered the holy places of the earthly Tabernacle, it points out that they are mere copies of the true holy places; the true Holy Place is heaven itself, the very presence of God (9:24).

Verse 20. In context, the "new and living way" into the

presence of God that Jesus has "consecrated" for us stands in obvious contextual contrast to the "old" and "dead" way of the law of Moses. (See 8:13; 9:8-10, 14; 10:1, 4, 9, 11.) It is "new" because it is based on the new covenant. (See 8:6-12.) It is "living" because this way is actually a living person, Jesus Christ, who imparts life. (See John 14:6.) That is, this way is not based on the blood of dead animals, but on the blood of one who was slain but is now alive forevermore. (See Revelation 1:18; 2:8.) The law of Moses was the "ministry of death" (II Corinthians 3:7, NKJV), but the Spirit that accompanies the new covenant gives life (II Corinthians 3:6-11). The old covenant separated people from God by declaring them to be sinners (Romans 7:5-13; Galatians 3:19-25); the new covenant brings them into fellowship with God by providing a means for their sins to be forgiven (verses 10, 14, 17-18).

Jesus "consecrated" this new and living way for us. The word translated "consecrated" (Greek, *enekainisen*) is simply the language of inauguration.[40] The same word is used in 9:18 of the old covenant, where the KJV translates it "dedicated." The inauguration of this new and living way overrides and terminates the inauguration of the old way, the law of Moses. They cannot coexist. (See comments on 8:13; 10:9.) Inauguration implies the beginning of a new administration, and that is exactly what Jesus Christ accomplished.

The statement that Christ consecrated this new and living way "through the veil, that is, His flesh" (NKJV) has been the subject of much speculation. Some have suggested the point is that His flesh (i.e., human nature) was a veil which obscured His deity. But this seems to impose a meaning on the verse. Rather, the language seems to continue the symbolism of verse 19 and may allude to the rending of the veil in the Temple at the moment of Christ's death (Matthew 27:51; Mark 15:38; Luke 23:45). In this sense, the veil is not a barrier to entry into the Holiest Place; the torn veil provided free passage into the Most Holy Place. Likewise, the flesh (i.e., "the body of Jesus Christ," verse 10), pierced on the cross, provides access into the true Holiest of All. The humanity of Jesus is not a barrier to intimacy with God; it is the means by which He stands in solidarity with us as our high priest (verse 21), thus enabling us to enter into the most intimate relationship with God.

If the veil here does not allude to the rending of the Temple veil but refers simply to the function of the inner veil in the Tabernacle in guarding the way to the Most Holy Place, the verse still indicates that it is through the flesh, or human nature, of Jesus that we have a way into the presence of God. The veil still is not a barrier. On the Day of Atonement, it was no barrier. There was a legitimate provision for entry beyond the veil. Just as the veil opened a way into the Most Holy Place on the Day of Atonement, so the sacrifice of the body of Jesus Christ opened the way into the presence of God as He atoned for the sins of the world on the cross.

Verse 21. Here is the final reference in the Book of Hebrews to Jesus as High Priest, thus forming a literary parenthesis with 2:17, the first mention. When we compare Moses' faithfulness *in* the house of God (3:2, 5) and Jesus' faithfulness *over* His own house (3:3-4, 6) with the statement that Jesus is "a high priest over the house of God," we find a strong indication of the deity of Jesus

Christ. In His identity as "Son," Jesus is "over His own house" (3:6); in His identity as "high priest," He is "over the house of God." Though we must not draw too sharp a distinction between "Son" and "high priest" (both terms assume His humanity), to think of Jesus as the Son of God is of necessity to think of Him as God, while to think of Him as High Priest is to focus on His solidarity with the human race.

In Hebrew thought, the concept of "son" indicates likeness. This thought underlies the identification of James and John as "sons of thunder" (Mark 3:17) and Barnabas as the "son of consolation" (Acts 4:36). When Jesus claimed that God was uniquely His Father, and by implication that He was thus the unique Son of God, the Jews understood Him to claim equality with God (John 5:18). From a Western perspective, we may think that likeness to God could mean similarity but something less than identity. Since God is unique, however, to be exactly like Him—or to be His Son in the sense Jesus claimed to be— is to be deity. If Jesus is not God, His claim is blasphemy and an encouragement to idolatry. As the Son of God (i.e., God manifest in flesh, I Timothy 3:16), Jesus is over His own house. As High Priest, He is over the house of God, the congregation of believers. (See discussion on 3:1-6.) As the Son of God, He is identified with God; as the High Priest, He is identified with us.

As the High Priest *over* the house of God, Jesus represents us to God by means of His atoning work. (See comments on 2:17; 3:1; 4:14-15; 5:5, 10; 6:20; 7:26; 8:1; 9:11.)

Verse 22. The high priesthood of Jesus enables us to draw near to God "with a true heart in full assurance of faith." To the original readers of this book, this remark was an exhortation to seek intimacy with God on the basis of Christ's high priestly work rather than on the basis of the law of Moses. Rather than "drawing back" (verse 39) from Christ and rejecting the work of the Cross (verse 29), believers must approach God with the full assurance which springs from faith that the blood of Jesus is God's exclusive answer to the sin problem (verse 19). A heart that has confidence in Christ alone is a "true heart" as opposed to an "evil conscience" that questions the efficacy and finality of His sacrifice.

When one's faith is in Jesus Christ alone, his heart is "sprinkled from an evil conscience," and his body is "washed with pure water." Here we find new covenant language: "Then I will sprinkle clean water on you, and you shall be clean; I will cleanse you from all your filthiness and from all your idols" (Ezekiel 36:25, NKJV). The original readers of this letter would have understood these words to say, "You have received the cleansing from sin promised by the Hebrew prophets to accompany the new covenant." (See verse 17.)

Some may suppose that the statement "our bodies washed with pure water" is a reference to water baptism, but this view is unlikely. The significance of water baptism is not in washing the body (I Peter 3:21). Nowhere is there any suggestion that the water of baptism is "pure" water. "Having our hearts sprinkled" is obviously a symbolic way of saying, "Our sins are forgiven." In this context, "having . . . our bodies washed" means the same thing. In light of the emphasis in Hebrews on the law as symbol for new covenant realities, there may be an allusion here to the ritual washing of the priests in the laver.

What their washing merely symbolized has been accomplished by the blood of Jesus.

In the context, an "evil conscience" is one that is not cleansed from sin and that continually reminds one of his sinfulness (verses 2-3). It is a conscience that relies on the law of Moses, or anything other than the blood of Jesus, to deal with sin and to gain access to the presence of God.

Verse 23. Here is the second of three closely related exhortations. The KJV translates this verse, "Let us hold fast the profession of our faith without wavering; (for he is faithful that promised)." The word translated "faith" here is *elpidos*, which means "hope." Thus the NKJV translates the verse: "Let us hold fast the confession of our hope without wavering, for He who promised is faithful." This phrase gives us a strong indication of the purpose for which the letter was originally written. The first Jewish readers were in danger of abandoning their hope in Christ Jesus as they contemplated a return to the rituals of the law of Moses. Such a step would have been spiritually disastrous for them. (See verses 26-39.) Rather than turning away from Christ, they needed to firmly retain the hope that springs from His atoning work. (See Romans 8:24-25.) They were to be unwavering in this hope; even to consider a return to the shadowy figures of the law of Moses was to betray the One who is faithful to keep His promises. Hope is the anchor of the soul (6:19).

It may be that the social pressures on the first-century Jews who believed on Jesus as their Messiah (see 12:3-4), the delay in Messiah's return, and the apparent continuing prosperity of the law of Moses as evidenced in the daily rituals of the Temple in Jerusalem all combined to cause them to waver in their hope and their confession. But to turn away from Christ for these or any other reasons is to act prematurely; He will keep every promise He has made to those who believe on Him. We must not forget that the new covenant is based upon "better promises" than the law of Moses (8:6).

The reference to "hope" here follows the reference to "faith" in verse 22 and precedes the reference to "love" in verse 24, thus bringing the letter to the Hebrews into conformity with the general emphasis on these three qualities in the New Testament epistles. Together, faith, hope and love represent the highest expression of the Christian life.[41]

Verse 24. Continuing the summary begun in verse 19, the letter exhorts its readers not to turn away from faith in Christ (verse 22) or from the hope that characterized their initial confession (verse 23), but to "consider one another in order to stir up love and good works" (NKJV).

The letter to the Hebrews offers a detailed doctrinal defense of the new covenant and its superiority over the old covenant. But doctrinal truth alone will not guarantee conformity to Christian character. In addition to recognizing the superiority of Jesus over all else—including the prophets of old, the angels, Moses, Aaron, and Joshua, as discussed in the early chapters of this book—the Jewish Christians needed to reaffirm and refresh the faith, hope, and love that had characterized them when they first believed. Specifically, as it pertained to love, they needed to stop focusing on the outmoded Temple rituals with nostalgic longings, and they needed instead to focus on the needs of one another for the specific purpose of stirring up love and good works.

In this trilogy, as in many other cases (e.g., I Corinthians 13:13), faith, hope and love are mentioned in this order. Though all three qualities abide, love is the "greatest." Where there is love for God, faith and hope will follow. Where there is love for one's fellow man, the same qualities will be evident. Those who love others will tend to trust them, and trust is the essence of faith. Those who love others will tend to hope for the best for and from those they love. (See I Corinthians 13:4-7.)

This is only the second time the word "love" is found in Hebrews. In the earlier mention, as here, love is tied to the qualities of faith and hope. (See comments on 6:10-12.)

Not only were the Hebrews to encourage each other to love, they were also to encourage one another to good works. Love is not merely a feeling. Just as genuine faith issues in works (James 2:14-26), so genuine love results in loving actions. The writer of Hebrews was opposed to "dead works" (6:1; 9:14), but not to the "good works" that spring from love for God and other people. The works of the law were dead in that the purpose for those rituals had now ended. There is always a place, however, for loving deeds.

There is no idea here that faith, hope, and love are merely psychological perceptions. Genuine faith results in drawing near to God (verse 22). Genuine hope results in unwavering allegiance to God (verse 23). And genuine love results in loving deeds performed both for God and others (verse 24).

The word translated "provoke" (or "stir up" [NKJV]) is a strong one (Greek, *paroxysmos*). In Acts 15:39 it is translated "contention." Generally, it has the idea of some kind of irritation. (See Acts 17:16; I Corinthians 13:5; Ephesians 6:4.) Its use here in a positive sense is striking and makes this exhortation all the more significant. The command is no casual one; believers are to vigorously promote love and good works in one another.

The most effective way to stir up another person to love and good works is by taking the initiative to love that person and to do good things for that person. When we are loved, we tend to love in return. When we are blessed by the good deeds of another, we tend to reciprocate by sharing the blessing of those good deeds with others. In other words, we are not so much stirred up by vocal admonition as by the example of love and good works in others.

The word translated "consider" (Greek, *katanoeo*) contains the idea "to pay attention to." It appears in 3:1, which urges believers to focus their attention on Christ Jesus. In view of the temptation the first-century Jewish believers faced to defect to the old covenant, "there may be a suggestion of watching out for possible failures or weaknesses in the community . . . though not with [an] unfriendly motive. . . ."[42] Verse 25 makes this thought especially likely. (See also 12:15.) Believers are to be alert to the spiritual struggles of their brethren. (See James 5:19-20; Galatians 6:1.) Rescuing one who is in danger of losing his faith is as important as his initial salvation.

Verse 25. One of the first and most visible signs of the Christian faith is the frequent gathering of believers for worship and mutual encouragement. (See Acts 2:42, 44-47.) Early in the Christian era, it was common for Jewish believers to gather for these purposes in synagogues. (See Acts 9:2, 20; 13:5, 14-15, 42; 14:1; 17:1, 10, 17;

18:4, 7-8, 19, 26; 19:18; 22:19; 26:11.) It was not until later in the first century, around A.D. 80-90, that the confession of faith required of all who frequented the synagogues was amended to include an article that amounted to blasphemy against Jesus Christ. The article was specifically intended to root out Jewish Christians from the synagogues. Even James, who wrote what is probably the oldest book in the New Testament, referred to the place of Christian worship as the synagogue (James 2:2).[43]

Just as frequent gatherings are indicative of the Christian faith, so where faith wanes it is characterized by a loss of commitment to the community of worship and exhortation. As this verse notes, some Jewish Christians had already forsaken the assembling of themselves together. There is something about belief in Jesus that thrives in mutuality. It is not meant to be experienced in isolation. When people choose isolation, it is the sign of a deeper spiritual crisis.

The writer of Hebrews urged these early Christians not to fall victim to the destruction of isolation from the community of believers. There is strength in the exhortation that arises from fellowship. The importance of faithfulness to the Christian assembly increases "so much the more as you see the Day approaching" (NKJV).

Significantly, this verse demonstrates the expectation of the early church for the return of the Lord. Everywhere in the New Testament, believers anticipate the Lord's return at any time. (See I Corinthians 15:51; I Thessalonians 4:15, 17; Titus 2:13; Hebrews 9:28.) The reference to "the Day," like "the day of the Lord" and "the day of Christ," is eschatalogical; these terms describe some aspect of the events associated with the return of Jesus.

(See Acts 2:20; I Corinthians 1:8; 5:5; I Thessalonians 5:2; II Peter 3:10.)

That believers can "see the Day approaching" indicates there are discernible signs of the Lord's return. Jesus said one of the signs of the end would be persecution. (See Matthew 24:9.) It may be that the writer of Hebrews referred to such persecution here. (See verse 32; 12:3-4.) If these early Jewish Christians were experiencing persecution for their faith, it was no time to consider giving up and returning to Judaism; the persecutions themselves were indications of the validity of their faith and of the approach of the time when their faith would receive its ultimate reward.

Verse 26. Verses 26-31 have been especially troubling to many who have not understood their meaning in the larger context of the Book of Hebrews. Some have interpreted these verses to mean that if a person sins after he is saved, there is no hope for his salvation. That is not at all the meaning of the passage.

In this entire section of exhortation, the writer of Hebrews included himself as needing to share in the reaffirmation and renewal he recommended to his readers. (See verses 22-25.) He included himself among those for whom Jesus had consecrated the new and living way (verse 20). Verses 26-31 are no exception. He did not identify with his readers in the positive expressions of Christianity only to abandon them in the warnings against apostasy. He wrote, "For if *we* sin willfully after we have received the knowledge of the truth, there no longer remains a sacrifice for sins" (NKJV). Here was a Hebrew Christian writing to Hebrew Christians. What was a danger for one was a danger for all. Gentiles, who were never associated with the law of Moses, could be tempted in many areas, but any temptation to identify with the dead rituals of the law would be minimal. But because of their long association with the old covenant, not only in a religious but also in a cultural sense, Jewish Christians must ever be alert to the danger of sacrificing the integrity of the new covenant on the altar of old covenant forms.

In the context, the willful sin warned against here is a defection from Jesus Christ and the new covenant to the dead works of the law. (See verses 9, 16-17, 20, 29, 32, 35, 39; 6:4-6; 8:6-13.) The "knowledge of the truth" these Hebrew Christians had received was the knowledge of the new covenant established in the blood of Jesus Christ as the fulfillment of all the prophecies of the Hebrew prophets about a coming covenant that would result in the remission of sins. (See verses 16-18.)

The phrase "there no longer remains a sacrifice for sins" has troubled many who suppose it means "there is no more forgiveness for sins." But that is not the meaning of this statement. The point is that for those who reject the sacrifice of Jesus, there is no other sacrifice that can atone for their sins. (See verse 18.) The sacrifices of the old covenant were no longer meaningful (8:13; 10:5-9), and even when they were in vogue they never took away sins (verses 4, 11). There is certainly no non-Christian sacrifice that can atone for sins. Therefore, those who turn away from the provisions of the new covenant are without any resource to deal with the problem of sin.

For the early Jewish Christians to turn away from Jesus Christ would have been a willful sin; they would have been sinning against the knowledge of the truth they had received. They had been illuminated (verse 32); their eyes were opened to the truth that Jesus was the promised Messiah. To turn from Him now would have been a purposeful, intentional, and arrogant move. There was no real question in their minds as to whether Jesus was the promised One. Their problem was apparently not one of understanding but of willingness to stand fast in the face of the pressures they faced from their brothers in Israel who had rejected the Lord (verse 33).

The word translated "sin" (Greek, *hamartanonton*) is a present active participle. It does not have to do with a one-time sin, or even an occasional sin, but with continual, persistent sin. The warning here is not against the struggles with faith that all Christians experience, or even the occasional lapse of faith that may occur, but against an ongoing rejection of Jesus. Those who reject Him will find no other source of salvation.

Verse 27. All that awaits those who reject Jesus is "a certain fearful expectation of judgment, and fiery indignation which will devour the adversaries" (NKJV). (See verses 30-31, 38-39.) This verse declares the exclusivity of Christianity. The gospel is not *a* way to salvation; it is the only way. At the second coming of Jesus, those who do not know God and those who do not obey the gospel of Jesus Christ will suffer the vengeance of God "in flaming fire." They will "be punished with everlasting destruction from the presence of the Lord and from the glory of His power" (II Thessalonians 1:8-9, NKJV). In this case, His "adversaries" are apparently those who have known Him (verse 26), but who have stubbornly turned away from faith in Him.

This description of the fate of those who turn away from Christ is startling and bleak, but it is true, and its purpose here to impress upon the reader the utter devastation that awaits those outside of Christ. It also underscores that the old covenant is no longer a viable option. It is not merely an inferior covenant; there is no salvation in it. We find salvation exclusively in the blood of Jesus (verse 19), the only way to God.

Verse 28. The first readers of this letter were quite aware of the penalty for rejecting the law of Moses. If two or three witnesses testified to having personal knowledge that anyone in Israel was guilty of worshiping false gods, the idolater was to be mercilessly stoned to death. (See Deuteronomy 17:2-7.) But this fate was mild compared to what awaited those who rejected the "new and living way" Jesus had inaugurated (verse 20). We see the superiority of the new covenant over the old covenant even in the penalty for the rejection of the covenant. Those who rejected the old covenant suffered the fate of physical death at the hands of their peers. But those who reject the new covenant will suffer the vengeance of God Himself (verses 30-31).

Verse 29. If the law of Moses required the death of those who rejected it, and it was merely a shadow of things to come (verse 1), then those who reject Jesus Christ are worthy of "much worse punishment" (NKJV). To reject Jesus after having received the knowledge of the truth (verse 26) and after having been illuminated (verse 32) is to trample the Son of God underfoot, to count His blood, upon which the new covenant is based and by which we are sanctified (verse 10), to be a common thing, and to insult the Spirit of grace (NKJV).

To trample Jesus underfoot is to reject Him as the promised Messiah. It is also to deny His deity, for such a rejection involves counting His blood to be common ("unholy" KJV), or just like the blood of any human. It is a rejection of the Atonement. The blood of Jesus was the blood of God (Acts 20:28). In a very real sense, then, to reject Jesus is to reject God Himself. The "Spirit of grace" is the Holy Spirit—God's Spirit characterized by the grace He imparts to believers. (See 4:16; 6:4; 12:15.)

Verse 30. Whereas those who rejected Moses' law were judged by humans and experienced the temporal punishment of physical death (verse 28), those who reject Jesus Christ and the new covenant in His blood will face the judgment of God Himself. This verse quotes portions of Deuteronomy 32:35-36, but the quote from Deuteronomy 32:35 does not precisely match either the Hebrew text or the Septuagint. In this case, the writer apparently had access to a Greek translation of the Hebrew Scriptures we no longer possess. This version of Deuteronomy 32:35 is witnessed to by the Targums, which are Aramaic paraphrases of the Hebrew Scriptures.[43] Apparently, more than one Greek translation circulated in the first century.

Including himself with his readers as he did earlier in this context (verses 20, 22-26), the writer declared, "We know Him who said." This statement would not have been appropriate to a Gentile audience who did not know the law of Moses. The Jewish author of this book, writing to a Jewish audience, shared with them a commonality of tradition. They understood each other.

In its original context in Deuteronomy, the statement "'Vengeance is Mine, I will repay,' says the Lord" emphasizes that judgment is a divine prerogative. The words are used to make the same point in another New Testament context (Romans 12:19). Here, however, the contextual emphasis is not that judgment belongs to God, but the severity of the judgment of God as compared to human judgment under Moses' law (verse 28). In this instance, the inspired New Testament writer used Old Testament words in a new way; the words find new emphasis in their new context. (See comments on 1:10.)

The second quotation in this verse, "The Lord will judge His people" (NKJV), is another example of Old Testament words receiving new meaning by their inspired use in a new context. In their original context, these words mean that God will vindicate His people; He will come to their defense "and have compassion on His servants" (Deuteronomy 32:36, NKJV). But in this new context, the judgment is one of condemnation of those who reject Jesus Christ. This judgment is fearful (verse 31).

The use of these quotations is significant for biblical hermeneutics (principles of interpretation). The same words can have different meanings, or at least different emphases, in different contexts. Thus context plays a crucial role in the interpretation of Scripture. Since each word of Scripture is inspired, the contexts are also inspired. Words are defined by their contexts. Given the right context, a word can take on a meaning radically different from the one it normally has.

For example, the New Testament ordinarily uses the word "image" (Greek, *eikon*) to refer to some kind of visible representation of someone or something, which can easily be distinguished from the person or thing represented. (See, for example, Mark 12:16; Romans 1:23; 11:4.) But in one context, the word refers to the reality itself. (See comments on 10:1.)

As another example, the New Testament quotes

Habakkuk 2:4 three times. In one context, the emphasis is on "faith" as opposed to the works of the law (Romans 1:17). In another context, the emphasis is on the "just," who live by faith, as opposed to the condemned, who are under the curse of the law (Galatians 3:11). And in Hebrews 10:38, the emphasis is that the just shall "live," as opposed to the perdition that those who "draw back" will experience (verse 39).

We must not take any statement of Scripture in isolation; God did not inspire the Bible as a series of disconnected statements or even in a chapter-and-verse format. He inspired it as a flowing narrative meant to be read in large, contextually-related segments. For this reason, "proof-texting," or the listing of widely separated verses that are thought to bear on the same subject in order to prove some point, can be dangerous. We should not cite verses in this way until we have carefully studied the context of each one to assure that they do indeed address the same subject. Some have cynically suggested that they could use the Bible to prove any point they wish, but they could do so only by ripping statements and verses from their contexts and giving them meanings that God and the human authors never intended.

Verse 31. People may have thought it a fearful thing to fall into the hands of human judges under the law of Moses (verse 28), but that judgment was mild in comparison to the judgment of those who trample the Son of God underfoot (verse 29). We see the superiority of the new covenant over the old covenant, a persistent theme in Hebrews, by the increased severity of judgment upon those who reject Jesus Christ. Just as there are degrees of reward in the eternal realm based on the quality of one's service in the kingdom of God (I Corinthians 3:12-15), so there are degrees of punishment based upon the extent of revelation one has rejected (Luke 12:47-48; Matthew 10:15). The increased severity of judgment for the rejection of Jesus Christ and the new covenant indicates that the revelation of the new covenant is superior to that of the old covenant. (See John 1:17.)

The same word translated "fearful" (Greek, *phoberos*) here also appears in verse 27. The point is that the prospect of judgment for who reject Jesus Christ is literally frightening. The prospect is frightening at least in part because, since the judge is God Himself, the judgment will be precisely appropriate. Under the law of Moses with its human judges, it was possible that a guilty person might go free. It was even possible that false witnesses could condemn an innocent person to death. But, at worst, the law provided for temporal punishment: physical death. But the judgment God will render at the last day will be eternal, and it will be according to the unmitigated facts as recorded in the heavenly books, including the "Book of Life" (Revelation 20:12-15). Those who stand before the Great White Throne will be judged not according to human testimony, which may be flawed, but according to their actual deeds.

The emphasis on the "living God" here contrasts with the deadness of the law (6:1; 8:13; 9:14). The law had served its purpose and no longer functioned as far as God was concerned. But the God who had given the law still lived, and He had now given a new and better covenant, which replaced the old.

Verses 32-33. The writer encouraged his original readers to recall the days when they first were "illuminated," or when they first came to know Jesus Christ as the promised Messiah. In order to regain the right perspective on their current temptations, it was necessary for them to refocus on the truth that first led them to turn from the rituals of the law and to place their faith in Christ alone. When they first turned to Christ, they boldly abandoned the Mosaic covenant and rejoiced in their newfound freedom. They did so even though they "endured a great struggle with sufferings" (NKJV) and even though they became a spectacle as they endured reproaches and tribulations. Not only did they endure these painful experiences themselves; they also "became companions of those who were so treated" (NKJV).

In other words, the first-century Jewish Christian community was a suffering community. Suffering was especially characteristic for Jewish believers because of the intense pressure they experienced from their families and friends who rejected Jesus and who viewed these new Christians as traitors to their faith. (See Matthew 10:32-37; Acts 4:1-22; 5:17-28, 40; 6:9-15; 7:54-60; 8:1-3.)

Though the original readers of this letter had suffered greatly for their faith, none of them had yet been martyred (12:4). This comment rules out Jewish believers in Jerusalem as the first recipients of this letter, for members of that church had begun to experience martyrdom as early as A.D. 33 with the stoning of Stephen. Again in A.D. 44, under Herod Agrippa I, James was beheaded.[44] But wherever there were Jewish communities in the first century, it was common for those who embraced Christ to experience the ridicule and disapproval of those who rejected Him.

Verses 34-35. During the earlier days of their faith in

Christ, the first readers of this letter had demonstrated compassion for the writer during his imprisonment. Some Greek manuscripts at this point read "for you had compassion on the prisoners" instead of "on me in my chains" (NKJV). Regardless of which reading is original, this comment is a continuation of the point made in the previous verse that they had become "companions of those who were so treated" (NKJV). During the time of the imperial persecution of the church, prisoners who had no means of personal support were allowed by their Roman guards to starve unless friends supplied them with food and other resources.[46]

Not only did the first readers of this letter demonstrate their compassion by ministering to those in prison; they also "joyfully accepted the plundering" (NKJV) of their goods. Though we do not know exactly how or when this plundering occurred, we have an account from Philo of similar events in Alexandria in A.D. 38 when the Jews of that city were evicted from their homes: "Their enemies overran the houses now left empty and began to loot them, dividing up the contents like the spoils of war."[47] The response of the Jewish Christians to such plundering was joy, because they knew they had "a better and an enduring possession . . . in heaven" (NKJV).

It seems obvious that the writer reminded his readers of their pristine faith and early experiences when their vision was clear in order to show them how far they had drifted in reaching a place where they actually considered turning away from faith in Christ to embrace the old ways all over again. There is a powerful lesson here for all believers: In order to retain our faith, we must continually refocus on Jesus Christ alone.

103

It is a terrible mistake for believers to cast away their confidence in Jesus Christ; there is great reward for such confidence. Although there are temporal benefits to trusting in Him, the ultimate reward is eternal. This eternal reward will cause any temporal discomfort to pale into insignificance by comparison.

Verse 36. The original readers of this letter had done the will of God when they were illuminated (verse 32) and placed their faith in Christ Jesus. When they retained their faith in the face of "great struggle with sufferings" (verse 32, NKJV), when they had compassion on imprisoned brethren, and when they accepted the plundering of their goods with joy, they had done the will of God. Now, they needed endurance so as not to forfeit the promise of God.

The larger context of the Book of Hebrews identifies "the promise" as the promise of eternal life that is included in the new covenant and that comes in conjunction with the "promise of the Father," the baptism of the Holy Spirit. (See comments on 9:15-17.) This is the promise that the people of faith in the era prior to the coming of the Messiah did not receive, even though they were justified by faith (11:39).

As people of faith, they will, of course, enjoy eternal life, but on the basis of the new covenant rather than any prior covenant (11:40). Since faith characterizes the new covenant, the benefits of the new covenant extend to people of faith who lived in the pre-Messianic era, just as the forgiveness from sin made possible by the blood of Jesus is given to those who lived prior to the Cross (Romans 3:25). In a sense, we can say that these new covenant benefits are made retroactive.

The lack of "the promise" does not mean that people of faith prior to the coming of Jesus died severed from fellowship with God, only to be restored to fellowship with Him after the work of the Cross. Since in the mind of God the work of the Cross, upon which the new covenant rests, was "from the foundation of the world" (Revelation 13:8), God was justified in declaring in advance the final judgment that He would pronounce upon the people of faith who lived and died before the coming of Jesus. Upon this basis, upon death those people entered into "Abraham's bosom," a Jewish idiom representing participation in the promises God made to Abraham, the most notable of which was justification by faith. (See Luke 16:22; Genesis 15:6; Romans 4:1-5.) Their status was anticipatory rather than final, for upon His ascension, Jesus "led captivity captive" (Ephesians 4:8), apparently taking those pre-Messianic people of faith who resided in "Abraham's bosom" and transferring them to paradise, or the "third heaven" (II Corinthians 12:1-4). The reference is not so much to spatial locations as to genuine events in the realm of the Spirit. In summary, even though people of faith in the Old Testament enjoy eternal life, they did not receive it on the basis of the law of Moses or of any covenant prior to the new covenant. They received it in a provisional sense in anticipation of the coming of Messiah.

The point of verse 36 is that to receive eternal life, one must not only begin in faith, one must endure in faith. This teaching cannot be harmonized with the idea of unconditional eternal security.

Verses 37-38. When it comes to faith in God, it is always too soon to give up. As the original readers of this letter contemplated casting away their confidence in

Jesus Christ, they were looking in the wrong direction. When they looked back over their shoulders at the law of Moses, the old covenant and the Temple rituals, they fixed their gaze on an outmoded and now-ineffectual system, rather than looking into the future and the certainty of the return of Jesus. (See Acts 1:11; James 5:8.)

The writer of Hebrews here made use of the words of Habakkuk 2:3-4 in a form varying from the Hebrew but similar to the Septuagint. (See comments on 1:10; 10:5-7.) From a human perspective, it may seem that the Lord is tarrying or delaying His coming, but He has established a precise time for this event, just as He did for His first entry into the world (Galatians 4:4; Mark 13:32). When that time comes, He will come without delay.

First-century believers anticipated His coming in their day ("yet a little while"). God has always allowed believers this wonderful hope; the time of His coming is His secret. If God had informed the first believers that He would not return for thousands of years, they would have had reason for despair, especially during periods of great persecution. On the other hand, in a very real sense, His return was to occur shortly, for with God a thousand years is as a day (II Peter 3:8).

Here appears one of three quotations of Habakkuk 2:4 in the New Testament. (See Romans 1:17; Galatians 3:11.) The prophet Habakkuk, when the law was still in force, declared that "the just shall live by faith." The point is that even under the old covenant, only people of faith were justified. It was not enough to perform the rituals of the law; the works of the law are powerless to justify, or to gain a person right standing with God. (See Romans 3:20.)

The contextual emphasis here is that people of faith enjoy life, and specifically eternal life, in contrast to those who "draw back to perdition" (verse 39). To draw back here means to turn away from Jesus Christ and the new covenant established in His blood. God takes no pleasure in those who reject Jesus.

Verse 39. Here, as in 6:9, we find a breath of fresh air. Though his warnings are uncompromising and stern, the writer of Hebrews was confident that the believers who comprised his original audience would not, in the final analysis, abandon Jesus Christ. Still including himself with his readers (see verses 20, 22, 23, 24, 25, 26, 30), he declared, "We are not of those who draw back" (NKJV).

He clearly asserted, however, that those who do draw back would face "perdition," which is translated from a Greek word (*apoleian*) that means destruction. Since those who commit this "willful sin" (verse 26) will experience the vengeance of God (verse 30) and fail to endure to the point of receiving "the promise" (verse 36), and since they are obviously not included in the "just" who enjoy "life" (verse 38), it seems evident that perdition describes the loss of their salvation and their ultimate spiritual destruction. As a further indication of this meaning, this verse contrasts drawing back to perdition with believing "to the saving of the soul" (NKJV). It is one thing to start out right (verse 32); it is another to endure to the point of receiving the promise of eternal life experientially and not just potentially. Those who ultimately receive the promise will be those whose faith endures to the Lord's return.

II.

Faith Is Our Only Approach to God
(11:1-40)

A. Faith Described
(11:1)

(1) Now faith is the substance of things hoped for, the evidence of things not seen.

Before plunging into a consideration of the nature of faith or specific examples of faith at work in the lives of "the elders" (verse 2), we must view this passage in the larger context of the entire letter.

The first-century Jewish Christians wrestled with the temptation to abandon a life focused on the unseen world in favor of a life focused on what was seen. Specifically, they were tempted to turn away from faith in Christ, who was no longer visibly and bodily present on earth, to return to the very visible sensory rituals of the law that emanated from the Temple in Jerusalem.

We should understand this section primarily as a call to refocus. While the law of Moses was fixed on visible and tangible things like the tables of stone and the Tabernacle (later the Temple) and its furnishings, the new covenant directs its gaze to things the natural eye cannot see. The central focus of the new covenant is the Messiah, who is present with us by means of His invisible Spirit. It also focuses on the new heart given to believers by the

Holy Spirit rather than on external conformity to the Mosaic code (Jeremiah 31:33).

The elders from Abel to the close of the Hebrew Scriptures "obtained a good testimony" (verse 2), but the law itself was "not of faith" (Galatians 3:12). It offered specific temporal rewards to those who did specific things. As we shall discover in this section of Hebrews, this description of the law does not mean that no one under the law had faith, which by definition means to believe in the unseen. That is precisely the point. It would have been senseless for first-century Jewish believers to abandon faith in Jesus Christ to return to an inferior covenant that depended upon the visible and tangible for its survival; even the Jewish elders who lived during the law's years of relevance were not justified by the works of the law but by faith in God. That included Moses, Joshua, Gideon, Barak, Samson, Jephthah, David, Samuel and many unnamed people. And in a brilliant stroke that must have been breathtaking to the first readers of this letter, this list of Hebrew heroes is sharply punctured by the inclusion of a Gentile, female harlot—Rahab—whose faith gained her equal standing even with the most revered of the Jewish champions.

We should view Hebrews 11 as illustrating the point of 10:38: "The just shall live by faith." To live a life that focuses on the visible world is to "draw back to perdition" (10:39). There is no place for compromise between a life of faith and a life that demands tangible assurance of God's presence in the form of predictable patterns (the Mosaic rituals) and outcomes. (See verses 35-38.) Faith demands no sensory reinforcement or cosmic concurrence with human ambition. It believes what it cannot see and trusts when it cannot understand.

Verse 1. As opposed to the tangible rituals of the law of Moses, faith is both substance and evidence. The Temple was standing in Jerusalem at the time of this letter, gleaming like a snow-covered mountain in the early morning sun. The sights and sounds of a rich tradition spanning many centuries emanated from its sacred courts. Everything about the Temple struck the human senses with powerful impact.

But the new covenant calls people, even Jews, away from fascination with ceremony and splendor to the simple life of faith in God. This faith itself is the "substance," not of things possessed, but of things "hoped for." In addition, faith is "evidence," not of things seen, but of invisible things. By contrast, a person could participate in the rituals of the law without faith. When the focus is on what someone already possesses and sees, faith can be absent. (See Romans 8:24-25.)

Some have misunderstood this verse to mean that faith is a force by which we can bring into existence things that do not presently exist but for which we hope. In addition, some think if we have faith, it is proof that the unseen things for which we are believing will one day materialize.

An examination of chapter 11 itself suffices to dispel these notions. Nowhere in the chapter does faith fit this description. Indeed, though all the people in this section had genuine faith, not one of them received faith's ultimate reward (verse 39). Instead, the faith described here is the human response to divine initiative. God speaks, whether with a specific or a general command, and men and women respond with obedient actions springing from their unquestioning trust in Him. That is faith.

Instead of teaching that by faith we can bring into existence things which do not exist, this passage teaches that there is an entire unseen realm not perceivable to the senses, but it is no less real because it is invisible. The same word translated "substance" here (Greek, *hypostasis*) is translated "confidence" in 3:14, which is the subjective, rather than objective, meaning of the word. *Hypostasis* literally means "that which stands under," in the sense of the foundation or essence of something.[48] Here it means that faith enables us to cling to the essentials of the new covenant, which, though not yet realized, already exist and will one day be clearly seen. The word translated "evidence" (Greek, *elegcho*) means "conviction," in the sense of something proven without doubt to be true.

The meaning of this verse is not mysterious. If we believe there is a God, though we have never seen Him, then we have faith. If we believe there is an unseen realm that includes angels, heaven, and hell, then we have faith. Faith does not demand sensory evidence; it is settled confidence in the unseen God.

B.

Faith Results in Justification
(11:2)

(2) For by it the elders obtained a good report.

Verse 2. The brief and clear statement of this verse should have convinced the original readers of this letter not to defect from the new covenant to return to the rituals of the law. If the "elders" (Greek, *presbyteroi*) "obtained a good testimony" (NKJV) through faith, their descendants should be convinced of faith's priority over ritual. The "elders" are those, both named and nameless, whom this chapter holds up for their examples of faith. On the basis of their faith, not on the basis of the law, they were justified (or gained right standing with God). (Compare verse 8 with Romans 4:3.)

C.

Faith Grasps the Testimony
of Scripture
(11:3)

(3) Through faith we understand that the worlds were framed by the word of God, so that things which are seen were not made of things which do appear.

Verse 3. The universe itself is visible, tangible, and perceptible to our sensory faculties. Thus, it requires no faith to accept the visible, created realm. It is there. We can touch it and see it. Only those who are deceived would deny its reality. But faith is necessary to understand that the visible realm was created by the word of God. Those who believe that "the things which are seen were not made of things which are visible" (NKJV) are people of faith. It is the absence of faith that causes some to deny the Creation accounts of Scripture. Where there is no faith, only what is tangible can be accepted as real.

This problem was precisely the one faced by the original recipients of the letter. The Temple was real; people could see it. The rituals were real; people could physically participate in them. The sights and sounds of the Temple Mount were real; people could perceive them by the senses. Their struggle was to accept as real what they could not see and what they had not yet realized. (See II Corinthians 4:18.)

This Creation account is in perfect agreement with all else Scripture has to say on this subject. The universe came into existence when God created the heaven and the earth (Genesis 1:1). The work of creation involved God speaking things into existence (Genesis 1:3, 6, 9, 11, 14, 20, 24). Thus, all things were made by the word of God. (See John 1:1-3; Psalm 29:3-8; 33:6, 9.)

Although "word" here is translated from the Greek *rhema*, while John 1:1 uses *logos*, there is no need to see a radical distinction between the two. Although *logos* has to do with both a thought and the thought expressed, while *rhema* focus more on the utterance itself, there is a substantial overlap of meaning between the two words. The influence of context on words is telling. Genesis describes God as speaking at Creation. Psalm 29 identifies the voice of the Lord with the Lord Himself. Psalm 33:6, 9 equates the word of the Lord and the vocalization of that word. Although John 1:1 personifies the Word, it does not suggest a plurality of persons in the Godhead any more than speaking of the life of God makes it a distinct person (I John 1:1-2).

Although this verse offers valuable insight on how the universe came into existence, that is not the primary reason the author wrote these words. His primary purpose was to point out that if his readers could believe that creation occurred by God's word—even though they had no first-hand, tangible evidence of how it occurred—they should also be able to retain their faith in the new covenant realities that the human senses could not yet perceive.

D.

Examples of Faith
(11:4-40)

1. Abel
(11:4)

(4) By faith Abel offered unto God a more excellent sacrifice than Cain, by which he obtained witness that he was righteous, God testifying of his gifts: and by it he being dead yet speaketh.

Verse 4. Working his way chronologically through the Hebrew Scriptures, the writer of Hebrews held up many examples of faith. These examples include not only those from the Mosaic era but also from before the law. They include not only men but women. And they include not only Jews but Gentiles. After reading this chapter, no one should doubt that faith is the only means of access to God.

The first example is Abel. (See Genesis 4.) Abel's sacrifice of the firstborn of his flock and of their fat was acceptable to God because he offered in faith. That is, Abel's offering was a result of his trust in God. Many conclude that God accepted Abel's sacrifice because it was a blood offering and rejected Cain's offering because it was not a blood offering, but Scripture does not clearly make this statement. This view is quite recent in the history of

Bible interpretation.[49] The Genesis account does not declare that these sacrifices were sin offerings. Indeed, the offerings seemed appropriate to the profession of each. Abel was a shepherd; he brought of the firstlings of his flock. Cain was a farmer; he brought an offering of the fruit of the ground.

In any case, it seems clear that God accepted Abel's offering because of his faith and did not accept Cain's offering because of his lack of faith. Indeed, before God respected Abel's offering, He respected Abel (Genesis 4:4). (See Matthew 23:35.) Before He rejected Cain's offering, He rejected Cain (Genesis 4:5). The reason God rejected Cain is that he did not "do well" (Genesis 4:7). (See I John 3:12.) If he had done well, God would have accepted him and, by implication, his offering also.

In this pre-Mosaic period, sacrifice was "acceptable to God not for its material content, but in so far as it [was] the outward expression of a devoted and obedient heart."[50] Cain's problem was sin (Genesis 4:7). The word translated "coucheth" by the KJV in Genesis 4:7 is cognate with the Akkadian name of a demon. Thus it pictures sin as an evil power "lying in wait to pounce upon its prey, but it is powerless against a man of righteous life."[51] Proverbs 15:8 sums up the situation well: "The sacrifice of the wicked is an abomination to the LORD, but the prayer of the upright is His delight" (NKJV). Regardless of the content of the sacrifice, it is an abomination to God if the person offering the sacrifice is wicked. That was Cain's fundamental problem.

The greatest difference between Cain and Abel is that Cain did not trust God while Abel did. Cain was very wrong to refuse to put his trust in God. Even though he blatantly insisted on coming to God on his own terms—which terms were not acceptable to God—God still loved him, appealed to him to do the right thing (Genesis 4:6-7), and assured that Cain would not suffer the violent fate he brought on his brother (Genesis 4:15).

Throughout this chapter we see that faith always results in some action or behavioral change. Faith cannot exist in a vacuum. It is not mere mental assent. Abel's faith resulted in the offering of a sacrifice to God.

We also see that faith is a person's response to God's initiative. It never begins with someone seeking divine endorsement. The idea to offer a sacrifice to God did not originate with Abel. He simply worshiped in a way God had already declared appropriate.

As with Abraham, who was counted righteous prior to circumcision on the basis of his faith alone (Romans 4:9-12), Abel was righteous (right with God) prior to his offering. In other words, he had genuine faith before he made his sacrifice. Indeed, it was his faith that prompted him to sacrifice. But this public demonstration of his faith by obedience gave God an opportunity to witness to Abel's righteousness. God did this by "testifying of his gifts" (NKJV). This testimony occurred when "the Lord respected Abel and his offering" (Genesis 4:4, NKJV).

Though Abel is dead, murdered by his rebellious brother, he "still speaks" by means of his primitive and powerful example. This point was particularly relevant to the original readers of this book. In a way, Abel was speaking to them, urging them not to abandon the life of faith for the life of ritual. In truth, Cain was the first ritualist. He was the first to seek access to God and approval from God on the basis of ritual apart from faith. Since ritual can be an expression of genuine faith only if God approves the ritual, the first-century Jewish Christians who contemplated a return to the rituals of the law would be guilty of the sin of Cain if they did so, for God no longer approved the rituals of the law as an expression of faith. They would thus be seeking God on their own terms. This self-willed approach may be the "way of Cain" in Jude 11.

Some have suggested that the phrase "he being dead still speaks" refers to the way in which Abel's blood still cries out for vengeance (Genesis 4:10). Without question, that is the point in 12:24. (See also Revelation 6:9-11.) But this verse does not mention the blood of Abel (it simply says that *he* speaks), and in the context the subject is not vengeance upon sin but the necessity of faith in approaching God. These points lead us to the interpretation just given.

2. Enoch
(11:5-6)

(5) By faith Enoch was translated that he should not see death; and was not found, because God had translated him: for before his translation he had this testimony, that he pleased God. (6) But without faith it is impossible to please him: for he that cometh to God must believe that he is, and that he is a rewarder of them that diligently seek him.

Verse 5. Enoch's translation demonstrates the dramatic power of faith. Enoch expressed faith in his simple walk with God (Genesis 5:22-24). Scripture tells us little about Enoch, but we do know that he was a prophet of God (Jude 14-15.) Enoch pleased God "*before* he was taken" (NKJV). Here again we see the nature of biblical faith. To be "taken away so that he did not see death" (NKJV) was not a goal Enoch had set. He was not believing for God to translate him, so that God was obligated to respond by doing the thing—however unusual—for which Enoch had faith. It was because he had faith and thus pleased God that God took Enoch.

The statement that "Enoch walked with God" (Genesis 5:24) gives us insight into the Hebrew view of the spiritual life. With our Western mindset, we interpret this statement to mean that Enoch *lived* for God, and of course he did. But in the Jews' view of life they literally, physically *walked with God.* In other words, instead of "walking with God" being something to do at special times or in special ways, it was simply one's conscious awareness of living all of life—whether worship, work, or play—in God's presence. There was no dichotomy between the sacred and the secular. All of life was sacred to God. Even the Hebrew word translated "work" (*abad*) includes the idea of worship. For those with faith in God, to plow a field was to worship God. People were to do everything for His glory and as unto Him.

Prior to the sin of Adam and Eve, God walked with them in the Garden of Eden (Genesis 3:8). To walk with God was to be in fellowship with Him. Since Enoch was a man of faith, he walked with God. By definition, to trust God is to walk with Him. We do not know why God translated Enoch and not others; God has not chosen to reveal that to us. But we do know that it was on the basis of his faith that Enoch received this blessing, not on the basis of ritualism.

Verse 6. It is impossible to please God apart from faith. This is the essential message the writer of Hebrews wished to communicate to his original readers. A life merely of adherence to the law of Moses is not a life of faith (Galatians 3:12). If they turned away from faith in Christ (6:6; 10:29) they would displease God, no matter how fervent or sincere their participation in Jewish ritualism. (See Galatians 1:14-16.)

To have faith is to come to God. There is no other approach to God than faith. Cain attempted to approach God through ritual alone (verse 4), but God rejected his attempt. The word translated "comes" (Greek, *prosechomenon*) has to do with worship. It conveys the idea of coming near to God in worship. Hebrews 10:1 use the same word in the phrase "make those who approach perfect" (NKJV), where the approach to God is under the sacrificial system of the law of Moses. The original readers of this book would have understood this connection. Under the law, people of faith approached God by the sacrificial system; under the new covenant, they approach God by faith without the sacrificial system, which has been fulfilled in Christ.

In this verse we find a practical definition of faith. Biblical faith has two components: (1) belief that God is, and (2) belief that He rewards those who seek Him diligently.

To believe that "He is" is to believe in the existence of the unseen God (11:1), with, of course, the understanding that it is the true God of Scripture in whom we believe. It is not enough to believe "a god" exists. The validity of faith depends completely on the object of faith. There is no power in faith itself; there is value to faith only if its object is the all-knowing, all-powerful God of the Bible who has revealed Himself in Jesus Christ. (See John 6:19; 14:1, 6.) Faith, or trust, is only as good as the one in whom we place the trust.

The phrase translated "He is a rewarder" (Greek, *misthapodotes ginetai*) can be more precisely translated "He becomes a rewarder." *Ginetai* is the present middle indicative of *ginomai*, which means "to become." The suggestion is that God responds to those who have faith in Him by rewarding their diligence in seeking after Him. In this context, to "seek Him" is to come to Him in worship.

The original readers of this letter surely had no problem believing in the existence of God, although some of them may have doubted the fullness of Christ's deity. (See 10:29.) If some of them struggled with Christ's preeminence and deity, that would explain why the writer consumed a substantial portion of his letter declaring the supremacy of Jesus Christ over all else, including the prophets of old, the angels, Moses, Joshua, and Aaron. It would explain the description of Jesus as the brightness of God's glory and the express image of God's person (1:3), as the One the angels worshiped (1:6), as the One declared to be God (1:8), and as Creator (1:10).

But regardless of their view of Jesus, it seems clear that the original readers of this letter struggled with the issue of the proper approach to God. This verse challenges their desire to defect from the new covenant and to go back to the old covenant way of worshiping God. They can no longer approach Him through the rituals of the law; they must abandon the shadow (10:1) and come to God on the basis of faith alone. And this faith must include the conviction that He will respond by rewarding their faith unaided by obsolete ritual.

3. Noah
(11:7)

(7) By faith Noah, being warned of God of things not seen as yet, moved with fear, prepared an ark to the saving of his house; by the which he condemned the world, and became heir of the righteousness which is by faith.

Verse 7. Noah is an example of how faith is convinced of the reality of "things not seen" (verse 1), for he responded to the divine warning of "things not yet seen" (NKJV). The idea to build an ark was not Noah's. He did not conceive a plan to build a boat and then trust God for a flood. The possibility of a world-wide flood would never have occurred to Noah. Instead, God warned Noah of the coming judgment and instructed him to build an ark (Genesis 6:13-22; 7:1-4). Noah's faith was demonstrated in his obedient response (Genesis 7:5).

The flood was not a divine response to Noah's faith; Noah's faith was a human response to a divine command. Noah responded with "godly fear" (NKJV); his faith was characterized by reverence for God.

The deliverance of Noah and his family from the destruction of the flood is an early example of salvation by grace through faith (Ephesians 2:8-9). Noah found grace in the eyes of the Lord (Genesis 6:8). The Hebrew word translated "grace" (*chen*) means "favor." When God graciously extended the offer of deliverance to Noah,

Noah responded in faith. Throughout the history of the human race, salvation has been received in this manner. When people respond in faith to the grace of God, salvation is the result.

The account of Noah indicates that salvation by grace through faith is not salvation by mental assent. That salvation is by grace does not preclude some requirement on the part of humans, and that salvation comes through faith does not preclude a specific response of faith. It was absolutely essential that Noah build a boat. This requirement does not mean that Noah was saved by works, however. Every moment of labor on the ark was an expression of his faith. Noah's confidence was in God, not in the boat. If Noah had not found grace in the eyes of God, he could theoretically have built a boat anyway, but God is able to sink any boat built by humans. There would have been no salvation in a boat built by human initiative; that would be salvation by works. But because Noah had faith, he obeyed God's command, and as a result of his obedient faith he received salvation according to the divine plan.

By his response of faith to God's command, Noah "condemned" or judged the world of his day. He proved that someone of his time and culture could have faith in God in the face of widespread corruption. If there had not been a Noah, it would seem difficult for God to have a just basis to judge anyone else. If not even one person on the face of the earth had been able to trust God during that time, it would seem that God was expecting the impossible. (See Romans 3:3-6.) Noah's faith, standing against the pervasive unbelief of his day, proved it was possible to trust God in the most difficult of times. Thus, no one could fault God for judging those who refused to believe on Him.

Noah "became heir of the righteousness which is according to faith" (NKJV). In other words, he was justified by faith. (See Genesis 7:1.) He was not justified by building the boat. Noah had faith prior to building the ark, and because of his faith he found grace in the eyes of the Lord. Thus he had right standing with God before God commanded him to build the ark. Because he was right with God, God shared with Noah His plan to destroy the human population while saving Noah's family.

4. Abraham and Sarah
(11:8-19)

(8) By faith Abraham, when he was called to go out into a place which he should after receive for an inheritance, obeyed; and he went out, not knowing whither he went. (9) By faith he sojourned in the land of promise, as in a strange country, dwelling in tabernacles with Isaac and Jacob, the heirs with him of the same promise: (10) for he looked for a city which hath foundations, whose builder and maker is God. (11) Through faith also Sara herself received strength to conceive seed, and was delivered of a child when she was past age, because she judged him faithful who had promised. (12) Therefore sprang there even of one, and him as good as dead, so many as the stars of the sky in multitude, and as the sand which is by the sea shore innumerable. (13) These all died in faith, not having received the promises, but having seen them afar off, and were persuaded of them, and

embraced them, and confessed that they were strangers and pilgrims on the earth. (14) For they that say such things declare plainly that they seek a country. (15) And truly, if they had been mindful of that country from whence they came out, they might have had opportunity to have returned. (16) But now they desire a better country, that is, an heavenly: wherefore God is not ashamed to be called their God: for he hath prepared for them a city. (17) By faith Abraham, when he was tried, offered up Isaac: and he that had received the promises offered up his only begotten son, (18) of whom it was said, That in Isaac shall thy seed be called: (19) accounting that God was able to raise him up, even from the dead; from whence also he received him in a figure.

Verse 8. The idea to leave Ur and to journey to Canaan did not originate with Abraham. God said to him, "Get out of your country, from your family, and from your father's house, to a land that I will show you" (Genesis 12:1, NKJV). By faith Abraham obeyed, even though he did not know the location of the land God would give him. Thus, he too is an illustration of faith's confidence in things "hoped for" and conviction of things "not seen" (verse 1).

With Abraham, the writer of Hebrews held up the example that would be most meaningful to his original readers. The Bible often offers Abraham as an example of faith. (See Acts 7:2-8; Romans 4:3; Galatians 3:6; James 2:23.) If Abraham could leave his home at the command of God, even without knowing his ultimate destination, surely the first-century Jewish Christians—physical and spiritual descendants of Abraham—could maintain their faith in Jesus even though they as yet had no tangible evidence of the ultimate new covenant promises. We must believe God's promises until their performance.

Initially, Abraham did not leave his home as a result of the assurance that he would inherit the land. The promise of inheritance came later (Genesis 12:7; 13:14-15; 15:18-21; 17:8). He obeyed God's voice purely out of his trust in God, not because of any incentive.

Like Noah, Abraham illustrates that faith is not mere mental assent. Abraham's faith resulted in his obedience. There can be no faith where there is unwillingness to obey the commands of God, whether those commands are to build a boat, leave one's home, or do anything else God directs. The commands of God may be general to all who live during a specific age, or they may be personal to an individual.

Verse 9. We see Abraham's faith not only in his initial response to God but also in his nomadic life "in the land of promise as in a foreign country" (NKJV). Even though he dwelt in the land that his heirs would eventually possess, neither he nor Isaac nor Jacob ever possessed it fully. (See Genesis 26:3; 28:13-15.) They lived in tents, moving from one place to another. (See Genesis 13:3, 18.) Abraham's trust in God was so complete that he did not demand the fulfillment of the promise in his lifetime. He was content with the confidence of hope.

The lesson for the original readers of Hebrews was that genuine faith does more than start the believer on his journey; it sustains him to the end. Just as Abraham had left Ur by faith, so the early Jewish Christians had begun their Christian life by placing their faith in the Messiah.

Now, just as Abraham had continued by faith to dwell in the promised land as a stranger, so they should sustain their profession of faith in Christ even though they suffered reproaches and tribulations (10:33). That Abraham was steadfast in his faith even though he never saw the fulfillment of all the promises God made to him should have encouraged Abraham's descendants, the Jewish people who believed on Jesus, to be unwavering in their faith, even though all their hopes had not yet been fulfilled.

Verse 10. Abraham's faith enabled him to see even beyond the promise of an earthly, temporal inheritance. Though it was still in the realm of unseen hope, he "waited for the city which has foundations, whose builder and maker is God" (NKJV). This phrase is not merely a description of the earthly Promised Land. "Many Jewish texts in Paul's day reinforced the Old Testament hope of a new Jerusalem, often speaking of a heavenly Jerusalem that would come down to earth. These texts also sometimes spoke of Jerusalem . . . as 'our mother.'"[52] Such references occur, for example, in the Dead Sea Scrolls.[53] The city in view here is a "heavenly" city (verse 16; 12:22; 13:14).

The "builder" (Greek, *technites*) of this city is God. *Technites* means a craftsman or designer.[54] God has designed the city. He is also the "maker" (Greek, *demiourgos*), the One who does the actual work.[55] This city owes nothing to human effort. It "has foundations." In the Greek text, the word "foundations" (*themelious*) is preceded by the definite article, meaning "*the* foundations." In other words, this city is the only one that has *the* foundations, or the eternal foundations.[56]

Hebrews does not suggest that Abraham had a fully developed understanding of this city to come. Indeed, the prophets of old did not understand much about the eternal future. (See I Peter 1:10-12; Ephesians 3:5.) But, since Abraham was a man of faith, he put himself in the company of all those who await faith's final fulfillment: the joys of the eternal state in the presence of God. No matter how vague Abraham's understanding of the heavenly city, it was to be his ultimate reward as a man of faith. All believers will one day enjoy the things "hoped for" and "not seen" (verse 1), not based on the level of revelation they have received (Abraham's revelation was certainly less than that of New Testament believers), but based on their faith.

Since Abraham patiently trusted God while waiting for unseen things, his descendants—the first-century Jewish believers—should be able to do the same. Though Abraham died without receiving the promises (verse 13), he never wavered in his faith (Romans 4:20). His example should encourage all believers to persevere in their faith in Christ even while they wait for faith's fulfillment.

Verse 11. Hebrews now moves from Abraham as an example of faith to his wife, Sarah, who was also an example. Physically, Sarah was incapable of bearing a child. (See Romans 4:19; Genesis 18:11-14). But because she trusted God that He would faithfully perform what He promised, she "received strength to conceive seed" (NKJV). Though we may not find a clear witness in the Old Testament to Sarah's faith, we may be sure that the record here is accurate. A great deal of information about the era of the patriarchs that was not written in the Hebrew Scriptures was transmitted from one generation to another by oral tradition. In addition, the writer of Hebrews was inspired by the Holy Spirit in this account.

Again we see that faith is a human response to divine initiative. The idea of having a child in old age was not Abraham's or Sarah's. Sarah was barren before God called Abraham out of Ur (Genesis 11:30). There is no record that Abraham or Sarah had asked God for a child. Though they may well have done so, there is certainly no indication that they had asked God for a child but wished to delay conception until they were very old and physically incapable of reproducing. As far as the biblical record is concerned, the first promise of God that Abraham and Sarah would have children appears in Genesis 12:2: "I will make you a great nation" (NKJV). The promise became more specific in Genesis 12:7: "Then the LORD appeared to Abram and said, 'To your descendants I will give this land'" (NKJV). Abraham was seventy-five years old at this time (Genesis 12:4). Since Sarah was ten years younger than Abraham, she was sixty-five (Genesis 17:17). For that time, they were apparently still within child-bearing age, for the average life-span of people in that day was much longer than today. Abraham was 175 years old when he died; Sarah was 127. So the promise that Abraham would have children probably did not seem miraculous when God first gave it.

In Genesis 13:15, the Lord reaffirmed to Abraham His promise to give him children. After ten years had passed and Abraham and Sarah were still childless, the Lord came to him in a vision and said, "Do not be afraid, Abram. I am your shield, your exceedingly great reward" (Genesis 15:1, NKJV). Abram responded, "Lord GOD, what will You give me, seeing I go childless, and the heir of my house is Eliezer of Damascus? . . . Look, You have given me no offspring; indeed one born in my house is my heir!" (Genesis 15:2-3, NKJV).

According to archaeological evidence, it was common at that time for wealthy couples who had no children to adopt a servant as their heir. God had promised to give the land to Abram and his descendants, but since he had no natural children and as far as he could see he would have none, Abram suggested that God might fulfill the promise by having him adopt Eliezer. At this time God made His promise more specific: "This one shall not be your heir, but one who will come from your own body shall be your heir" (Genesis 15:4, NKJV). Because Abraham believed this promise, right standing with God was accounted to him (Genesis 15:6).

Even after this promise, Abraham cooperated with Sarah in a scheme to father a child by Hagar (Genesis 16:1-4, 15-16). Abram was eighty-six years old at this time. At this point, then, it was Sarah who was unable to reproduce, not Abram. This error on Abram's part became the source of tension between the descendants of Ishmael and Isaac to this day.

Thirteen years later, when Abram was ninety-nine years old (Genesis 17:1), the Lord reiterated His covenant with Abram and made the promise of children even more specific: "As for Sarai your wife, you shall not call her name Sarai, but Sarah shall be her name. And I will bless her and also give you a son by her; then I will bless her, and she shall be a mother of nations; kings of peoples shall be from her" (Genesis 17:15-16, NKJV). God had already changed the name of Abram, which means "exalted father," to Abraham, which means "father of a great number" (Genesis 17:5). Sarah's name change seems less significant: Sarai means "my princess," while Sarah means "princess." The change to Sarah may indicate that she would no longer be a princess only in the eyes of Abraham, but because of her offspring, in the eyes of others as well.

Even at this point, however, Abraham responded by falling on his face, laughing, and asking in his heart, "Shall a child be born to a man who is one hundred years old? And shall Sarah, who is ninety years old, bear a child?" (Genesis 17:17, NKJV). Instead, Abraham again offered God an alternative: "Oh, that Ishmael might live before You!" (Genesis 17:18, NKJV). As with Eliezer, Abraham offered God a way to fulfill the promise of descendants without a miracle. But God responded, "No, Sarah your wife shall bear you a son, and you shall call his name Isaac; I will establish My covenant with him for an everlasting covenant, and with his descendants after him" (Genesis 17:19, NKJV). Isaac means "he laughs." God fulfilled His promise by supernatural intervention in spite of Abraham's laughter.

Then, when both Abraham and Sarah were "well advanced in age" and Sarah past the age of childbearing, the Lord appeared again to Abraham and said, "I will certainly return to you according to the time of life, and behold, Sarah your wife shall have a son" (Genesis 18:10-11, NKJV). Sarah was listening inside the tent, and as Abraham had done earlier, she "laughed within herself, saying, 'After I have grown old, shall I have pleasure, my lord being old also?'" (Genesis 18:12, NKJV). But, as God had said, Sarah did conceive and bear Abraham a son (Genesis 21:1-8).

Throughout this account, it is difficult to see the response of Abraham and Sarah as so strong in faith that they obligated God to fulfill their wish. Instead, from beginning to end, the plan and promise came from God, and He continued to lead Abraham and Sarah until they could fully believe, comprehend, and receive His promise.

How does this account fit with the description of Romans 4:18-20 that Abraham was not "weak in faith" and "did not waver at the promise of God through unbelief"? Abraham had no doubt that God would keep His promise to give him many descendants. But Abraham did not understand how it would happen, for he thought perhaps it would be through his servant Eliezer or, later, through his son with Hagar, Ishmael.

When we consider the entire account, it is clear that the faith of Sarah and Abraham to have a child in old age did not originate with them. Abraham attempted to convince God to fulfill His promise another way, and both of them expressed skepticism that the promised son would be born to them when they were past child-bearing age. Thus, their faith was a trusting response to God's initiative. Although Sarah had at first laughed, she did, in the final analysis, believe that God was able to do what He promised to do.

As with all the other "heroes of faith" in this chapter, Sarah demonstrated that faith is the confidence of things hoped for and the conviction of things not yet seen. (See verse 1). She believed God for the son she could not see, simply because God had promised the son to her.

Verse 12. Though Abraham was past the natural age of reproduction (Romans 4:19), God miraculously enabled him to father a son. This divine enablement was not temporary. After Sarah's death, Abraham took Keturah for a wife and fathered several children by her (Genesis 23:1; 25:1). Indeed, God fulfilled the promise that Abraham's descendants would be as innumerable as the stars of the sky and the sand by the seashore. (See Genesis 15:5; 22:17.) This statement does not mean that Abraham's descendants will literally equal in number the stars or the sand, but that, like the stars and the grains of sand, they will be so numerous that it will be impossible to count them precisely.

Early dispensationalists tended to say the sand represented Abraham's earthly descendants, the Jews, and that the stars represented his heavenly descendants, the church. Though there is a clear distinction between Israel and the church (I Corinthians 10:32), it is doubtful that the stars and the sand bear this significance. First, any Jewish person can enter the church on the same basis as any Gentile (Romans 11:17-24). Second, in the church ethnic distinctions are insignificant (Galatians 3:28; Colossians 3:11). Third, the church is a mystery not evident in the Hebrew Scriptures (Ephesians 3:1-6). The stars and sand simply illustrate the multitude of Abraham's descendants.

Verses 13-14. All of those mentioned so far in this chapter with, of course, the exception of Enoch, died in faith. At their death, they were still trusting God to keep His promises. The only promise mentioned contextually that was not fulfilled before their death is the promise that Abraham and his descendants would inherit the land from the Euphrates to the Nile (Genesis 15:18). Hebrews may refer to promises in the plural to point out that Abraham was not the only one to see death before realizing the fulfillment of all of God's promises to him. This is a common experience for people of faith. Just because some promises are not fulfilled in this lifetime, that is no indication they will not be fulfilled. There is a world to come.

Though people of faith died without receiving all the promises of God, they saw them "afar off." This phrase underscores the nature of faith. Faith is confident of things hoped for but not yet received, and it is convinced of things not seen. (See verse 1.) These people of faith embraced the unfulfilled promises with the confession that they were "strangers and pilgrims on the earth" (NKJV). This confession reveals their understanding of the temporal nature of this present earth and the certainty of life beyond. Their faith prevented them from viewing life on this earth as final. They were not discouraged if they did not see the fulfillment of every divine promise during their earthly life. Abraham, who waited for the only city with eternal foundations, was an example of this faith. (See verse 10.)

Those who confess the temporary nature of their stay on this earth testify plainly that they are seeking something beyond this world. People of faith are identified by their lack of attachment to this present world and their eager anticipation of the next; people of unbelief are identified by their attachment to this world and their view that this present life is all there is.

Verse 15. If Abraham had focused his attention on Ur, the country he left, opportunity would have presented itself for him to return to it. Likewise, if the original readers of this letter took their focus off Jesus and the new covenant and looked with longing back to their former life under the old covenant, the opportunity would present itself for them to turn away from Jesus to embrace the law all over again. There is a also warning here even to those who have never been under the law of Moses: If, after coming to Jesus, we focus longingly on the life we lived before coming to Him, we will find opportunity to turn away from our Lord. But to go back to life before the promise is to forfeit the promise through disobedience. The promise of God will come only to those who press on in its pursuit.

Verse 16. The persistent faith of the patriarchs is evidence that they were ultimately pursuing, not just an earthly inheritance, but a heavenly one. That is precisely what God has prepared. (See verse 10.) Since God has made preparation to reward their faith, He is not ashamed to be identified as the God of people of faith. Genuine faith will never go unfulfilled. God would be ashamed if He failed or refused to reward those who seek him diligently (verse 6).

Verses 17-19. Nowhere is the nature of faith better demonstrated than in the offering of Isaac by Abraham. Verse 17 declares, "By faith Abraham, when he was tested, offered up Isaac" (NKJV). The idea to offer Isaac as a burnt offering certainly did not originate with Abraham. (See Genesis 22:1-2.) God called Abraham to make this sacrifice, and Abraham's response demonstrated the depth of his unquestioning trust in God. Someone said, "Faith begins when God speaks." Abraham's faith was the confidence of things hoped for and the conviction of things not seen, for he concluded that if he offered Isaac, God was able to raise him up (verse 19).

God's call to offer Isaac was a test of Abraham's faith. It was not a temptation to sin, for God does not tempt anyone to sin (James 1:13-14). The use of the Greek *peirazo* both in James 1:13 and here illustrates that words are defined by their contexts. The context in James defines *peirazo* as temptation to sin that arises from one's own lust, while the context here defines it as a test from God, since Genesis 22:1, to which this verse refers, specifically reports that God "tested" Abraham (NKJV).

When people consider the offering of Isaac, they commonly focus on the inner turmoil of Abraham as he set out to obey God. But not only is the Old Testament account silent about any such turmoil, that is not the focus here. The point here is the challenge that faced Abraham to reconcile God's promise with God's command. Abraham knew without question that Isaac was the promised son through whom God would fulfill His promise to make Abraham the father of many nations. (See Genesis 17:19, 21; 21:12; Romans 9:7.) Now God had commanded him to offer Isaac as a burnt offering. How could Isaac die and still be the son through whom God would fulfill His promises to Abraham?

Abraham's trust in God on this point was unquestioning. He knew that if he offered Isaac, God would raise him from the dead, for that was the only way God could fulfill his promises to Abraham through Isaac. Indeed, "in a figurative sense" (verse 19, NKJV), Abraham did receive Isaac back from the dead, because as far as Abraham was concerned, Isaac was offered. The word translated "offered up" in verse 17 (Greek, *prosenenochen*) is in the perfect tense, which indicates the action was completed in the past with the effects of the action continuing into the present. Abraham did not anticipate that an angel would interrupt the sacrifice of Isaac (Genesis 22:10-12). Had he not been interrupted, he would certainly have completed the sacrifice with the full assurance that God would raise Isaac from the dead.

But the actual performance of the sacrifice was not to be. The phrase in the latter part of verse 17 that "he who had received the promises offered up his only begotten son" (NKJV) makes use of the Greek *prosepheren*, translated "offered," which is in the imperfect tense. It indicates that Abraham was in the process of offering up his son, but it does not declare that the offering was finalized.

Since Abraham received Isaac back from the dead "in a figure," it may be that this entire episode in the life of Abraham foreshadowed the sacrifice of Jesus Christ and His resurrection from the dead. Verse 19 uses the Greek *parabole*, translated "figure," which may suggest that the events of Moriah were a parable. The word *parabole* refers to something thrown alongside something else for the sake of comparison. John 3:16 uses the Greek *monogene* ("only begotten") of Jesus, and this passage uses it of Isaac. Although Abraham had already fathered Ishmael, Isaac was his "only begotten son" as pertaining to the promise of God. Ishmael, the son resulting from Sarah's scheme and Abraham's natural strength, had no part in the Abrahamic covenant.

If the offering of Isaac is a parable of the giving of the only begotten Son of God, this event may be what Jesus referred to in John 8:56: "Your father Abraham rejoiced to see My day, and he saw it and was glad" (NKJV).[57]

James 2:21 also appeals to the account of Abraham's offering of Isaac as evidence of the genuineness of Abraham's faith.

5. Isaac (11:20)

(20) By faith Isaac blessed Jacob and Esau concerning things to come.

Verse 20. Isaac, the son of promise, was also a man of faith. Although Esau sold his birthright to his brother Jacob and later lost the primary blessing of their father through Jacob's deceit (Genesis 25:27-34; 27), he was still the recipient of a blessing. Isaac blessed both Jacob and Esau, and he pronounced these blessings by faith. (See Genesis 27:24-40.) Esau's subservient position was not due to any prejudice on the part of his father or God. He was a profane person who devalued his birthright (Hebrews 12:16).

Isaac's blessing was by faith in that it concerned things to come, or things hoped for but not seen. (See verse 1.) These blessings did not spring from Isaac's imagination; they were not a product of his wishful thinking. Since we know that the blessing he pronounced on Jacob was according to the will of God, in spite of the deceit of Rebekah and Jacob, it follows that the more limited blessing he pronounced upon Esau was also in accordance with God's will.

In Isaac's response to Esau, we see his recognition that Jacob was the rightful recipient of the blessing God intended: "I have blessed him—and indeed he shall be blessed" (Genesis 27:33, NKJV).

6. Jacob (11:21)

(21) By faith Jacob, when he was a dying, blessed

both the sons of Joseph; and worshipped, leaning upon the top of his staff.

Verse 21. In Jacob's final blessing upon the sons of Joseph, we continue to see the role of faith in the preservation of the promise God first made to Abraham, then extended to Isaac, and then to Jacob. The last words of the family patriarch before death had great significance. (See Genesis 48.) Jacob's blessing of Ephraim and Manasseh was not mere tradition. Against Joseph's wishes, Jacob placed his right hand on the younger Ephraim, conferring the greater blessing upon him. (See Genesis 48:13-20.) He did so by faith: the blessings he pronounced involved things hoped for but not yet seen. (See verse 1.) By definition, the faith that prompted Jacob to perform the unusual act of crossing his hands when laying them on Joseph's sons was his trusting response to God's direction. The idea of making such a distinction between the two was not Jacob's.

The statement that Jacob "worshiped, leaning on the top of his staff" is a reference to Genesis 47:31, where Jacob "bowed himself on the head of the bed" (NKJV). As usual, writer of Hebrews followed the Septuagint translation at this point. The question as to whether the translation should be "bed" or "staff" arises because the original Hebrew language was written without vowels. Only consonants were used; vowels were supplied orally when the Scriptures were read. In some cases, as here, by the insertion of different vowels, a word can mean more than one thing. The consonants of the Hebrew word translated "bed" are *mtth.* When the word is read *mittah*, as in the Massoretic text, it means "bed." When it is read *matteh*,

141

as by the translators of the Septuagint, it means "staff." One could argue from the inspiration of the New Testament that the reading *matteh* is correct.

Not only did Jacob bless Ephraim and Manasseh by faith, he also worshiped by faith. The account in Genesis 47:31 follows immediately Joseph's promise to Jacob that he would carry his body out of Egypt to bury him with his fathers (Genesis 47:29-30). Although at the time this promise was an unseen hope, Jacob was confident that it would come to pass, and in that confidence he worshiped. The basis of Jacob's faith was the promise God had made first to Abraham, then to Isaac, and finally to Jacob himself concerning their inheritance of the land. (See Genesis 12:7; 13:14-17; 15:18-21; 17:8; 26:1-3; 28:13-15; 35:11-12.) Jacob's trust that God would keep His promise was so complete that he knew his descendants would not remain in Egypt, and he wished to be buried in the land God had promised to him.

7. Joseph (11:22)

(22) By faith Joseph, when he died, made mention of the departing of the children of Israel; and gave commandment concerning his bones.

Verse 22. Like his father Jacob before him, at his death Joseph asked the Israelites to carry his bones out of Egypt and bury them in the Promised Land. (See Genesis 50:24-25.) By faith Joseph made his dying declaration about the future departure of the Israelites from Egypt. On the basis of the promise God had made to Abraham, Isaac, and Jacob that their descendants would inherit the land, Joseph knew that God would "surely visit" the Israelites to bring them out of Egypt to the Promised Land (Genesis 50:24-25). Thus, Joseph's faith illustrates his confidence of things hoped for and his conviction of things not seen. (See verse 1.) In accordance with his wishes and their oath to him, the Israelites did carry Joseph's bones out of Egypt in the Exodus. (See Exodus 13:19; Joshua 24:32.)

8. Moses' Parents (11:23)

(23) By faith Moses, when he was born, was hid three months of his parents, because they saw he was a proper child; and they were not afraid of the king's commandment.

Verse 23. After the death of Joseph a new king arose in Egypt who had not known him. (See Exodus 1.) He feared that the increasing numbers of Israelites would, in the case of war, assist the enemies of Egypt and vacate the land. This new pharaoh placed the Israelites under harsh forced labor and commanded the Hebrew midwives to kill any male children born to Hebrew women. Because of their fear of God, the midwives did not obey the command of the king. When the pharaoh inquired as to the reason for their failure to obey him, the midwives reported, "The Hebrew women are not like the Egyptian women; for they are lively and give birth before the midwives come to them." Because of their refusal to obey the king, God blessed these midwives while the Israelites continued to multiply and increase in might. Since he had been unable to limit the growth of the Israelite population

143

by infanticide, the pharaoh apparently broadened his command, commanding the Egyptians to cast every newborn Hebrew boy into the river.

At this point, Moses was born. His mother hid him for three months, and when she could hide him no longer, she "took an ark of bulrushes for him, daubed it with asphalt and pitch, put the child in it, and laid it in the reeds by the river's bank" (Exodus 2:1-3, NKJV).

From the account in Hebrews, we discover that the parents of Moses acted by faith in hiding the baby for three months. The focus at this point is not on the placement of Moses in an ark in the river, where the daughter of Pharoah found and rescued him (Exodus 2:5-10). Though that act was also one of faith, Hebrews reveals that the trust Moses' parents had in God was greater than their concern for the king's command to murder all newborn Hebrew boys. The faith of Moses' parents caused them to preserve this "beautiful child" (NKJV).

This adjective seems to mean more than physical beauty. The word translated "beautiful" ("proper," KJV) is the Greek *asteion*, which appears only here and in Acts 7:20, in both cases referring to Moses. The Jewish historian Josephus declared that God gave a vision in the night to Moses' father, Amram, to tell him that Moses was no ordinary child but was destined by God to accomplish great things for His people.[58] The Talmud includes a similar account, speaking of a revelation to Miriam, Moses' sister, in her role as a prophetess.[59] In his commentary on this verse, John Calvin wrote that the issue was not any external beauty Moses possessed, but a "mark, as it were, of future excellency imprinted on the child, which gave promise of something out of the ordinary."[60]

We might dismiss these traditions as fancy except that this verse specifically asserts that Moses' parents hid him "because they saw he was a beautiful child," in keeping with Exodus 2:2. It would seem very strange if the only reason they hid him, sparing him from death, was because of his physical appearance. Would they have submitted to Pharaoh's command if the baby had been less beautiful? No doubt many Hebrew parents risked their lives to spare the lives of their newborn sons. That does not seem to be the point here. Certainly, if they were people who feared God, Moses' parents would not have obeyed the command to kill him under any circumstance. But in this case, their disobedience to the king's command is credited to something unusual. They saw something in the baby that motivated them, even beyond parental love, to spare his life.

Stephen's account makes clear that something was unusual about the baby: "At this time Moses was born, and was well pleasing to God; and he was brought up in his father's house for three months" (Acts 7:20, NKJV). The same word translated "beautiful" in Hebrews is translated "well pleasing" in Acts. But in Acts, Stephen declares that Moses was well pleasing *to God*.[61] Since, in a sense, all children are beautiful to God, this description must mean something more than that Moses was a beautiful baby. Moses was well pleasing to God even as a newborn infant during the first three months of his life. This status had nothing to do with Moses' own faith, which he would exhibit later. All of these descriptions strongly suggest that something alerted the parents that God had chosen this baby for a specific and significant work. In this case, as in Jude 14-15, it may be that Jewish tradition preserved a historical narrative not recorded in Scripture.

The example of Moses' parents indicates the appropriateness of civil disobedience when obeying the command of a human authority would mean disobeying God. (See Acts 4:19-20; 5:27-29.) Generally, Christians are to obey those in civil government (Romans 13:1-7). But when the civil government issues orders contrary to the commands of God, there is no choice but to obey God, disobey the human order, and accept whatever consequences may come. (See Daniel 3.) Scripture reveals that God will sometimes bless this course of action by protection from the wrath of the offended human authority. But it also indicates that God does not always do so (verses 35-37).

In the case of Moses' parents, there is no indication that they had special assurance from God that He would spare them from Pharaoh's wrath. But even without this assurance, they trusted God and did not fear the king. In this case, it was the will of God to spare their son and them as well from any human penalty.

9. Moses (11:24-29)

(24) By faith Moses, when he was come to years, refused to be called the son of Pharaoh's daughter; (25) choosing rather to suffer affliction with the people of God, than to enjoy the pleasures of sin for a season; (26) esteeming the reproach of Christ greater riches than the treasures in Egypt: for he had respect unto the recompence of the reward. (27) By faith he forsook Egypt, not fearing the wrath of the king: for he endured, as seeing him who is invisible. (28) Through faith he kept the passover, and the sprinkling of blood,

*lest he that destroyed the firstborn should touch them.
(29) By faith they passed through the Red sea as by
dry land: which the Egyptians assaying to do were
drowned.*

Verse 24. Not only were the parents of Moses people
of faith; Moses was a man of faith as well. The phrase
"when he became of age" ties this event to Exodus 2:11:
"Now it came to pass in those days, when Moses was
grown . . ." (NKJV). As he did throughout this book, the
writer of Hebrews followed the Septuagint here. The
words "became of age" are translated from the Greek
megas genomenos (literally, "having become great"),
which is identical to the Septuagint translation of Exodus
2:11. Stephen reported that Moses was forty years old at
this time (Acts 7:23).

Moses' refusal to be identified as the son of Pharaoh's
daughter relates to his rescue of a Hebrew man whom an
Egyptian was beating. Moses killed the Egyptian and hid
him in the sand. The next day, Moses came upon two
Hebrew men fighting and attempted to stop them. The
response of the wrongdoer revealed to Moses that his
actions of the previous day were public knowledge. When
the news reached Pharaoh that Moses had killed an
Egyptian, he sought to kill Moses. Moses fled to the land
of Midian. (See Exodus 2:11-15; Acts 7:23-29.) According to Stephen, Moses "supposed that his brethren would
have understood that God would deliver them by his
hand" (Acts 7:25, NKJV). Apparently, then, even at this
early point in his life, Moses had an awareness of his destiny to deliver the Israelites from Egyptian slavery.
Because he embraced this destiny, he had to reject his

identity as Pharaoh's grandson.

This act on Moses' part illustrates his faith in God. Even thought he was aware of his destiny as Israel's deliverer, this hope was not yet realized. Like all people of faith, however, Moses was persuaded of things hoped for and convinced of things not seen. (See verse 1.) Although his attempt to deliver one of his brethren was premature, he trusted that God would one day use him to set his people free.

Verse 25. Moses' choice to identify with his own people rather than with the Egyptians caused him to stand with the Hebrews in their affliction instead of enjoying "the passing pleasures of sin" (NKJV), which were his as a member of the royal household. There was a direct application to the original readers of this book who faced the temptation of apostasy. If the first-century Jewish Christians defected from their allegiance to Jesus Christ and the new covenant to return to the Temple rituals and the law of Moses, they would be like Moses if he had rejected the will of God for his life to cling to his previous life of privilege and prestige. The affliction they now experienced (10:32-33) contrasted starkly to their previous place of privilege in the Jewish community as did Moses' affliction with his prior exaltation. They too, like Moses, needed to be willing to "suffer affliction with the people of God" rather "than to enjoy the passing pleasures of sin." To reject Jesus as the Messiah (10:29) would be a sin even more awful than if Moses had rejected his role as the deliverer of his people.

Verse 26. Here is a fascinating example of the inspired application of an Old Testament event to a New Testament situation. Hebrews has Moses "esteeming the reproach of Christ greater riches than the treasures in Egypt" (NKJV). It may at first glance seem strange that the affliction Moses willingly embraced could be called "the reproach of Christ." He lived, of course, long before the Messianic era; indeed, he made his choice prior to the writing of any Scripture containing Messianic prophecies. The word "Christ," transliterated from the Greek *Christos*, is the Greek equivalent to the Hebrew *Messiach*; both words mean "anointed one." They refer specifically to Jesus the Messiah, the One anointed to deliver His people from their sins, who was not only a human being but also "God with us" (Matthew 1:21-23). Since the Incarnation was far in the future, how could Moses have had any awareness of the "reproach of Christ"? Even if he had some knowledge of a coming Messiah from revelation he personally received from God or from oral tradition harking back perhaps as far as the events of Genesis 3:15, how did he connect the events surrounding Israel's captivity in Egypt with this promise?

At this point, we must remember that revelation need not be complete for someone to believe it, nor must faith be aware of all the details and timing of God's plan in order to be real. The Israelites cried out to God for deliverance from the oppressive treatment they suffered at the hands of the Egyptians (Exodus 3:7-9; Acts 7:34-35). However near-sighted or limited their understanding, their cry for deliverance was a cry for a Messiah, one anointed by God to free them from bondage.

Israel's deliverer in the most immediate sense was Moses (Acts 7:34-35; I Corinthians 10:1-2). In this limited sense, Moses was their "Messiah." Perhaps the passage means that he esteemed the reproach of being Israel's deliverer more valuable than Egypt's treasures. As Israel's deliverer, Moses subjected himself to the rejection and ridicule of both Pharaoh and his own people. The NEB says Moses esteemed "the stigma that rests on God's Anointed" greater riches than the treasures in Egypt. He was the anointed of God for the Hebrews, a type of the ultimate Anointed One who would deliver all people not just from physical captivity, but from sin's slavery.

Trinitarian commentators, who believe God is three persons, typically understand the "reproach of Christ" differently. Some suggest that the author of Hebrews "thought of Christ as identified in some way with the people of God in [Old Testament] times."[62] According to this view, not only was the first person of the trinity involved with his people, so was the second person in some way. But from the perspective of Oneness theology, this notion is problematic. Even trinitarian theology holds that the supposed second person of the Godhead did not assume Messianic identity until the Incarnation. Therefore, to know "Christ" prior to the Incarnation, unless it was prophetically, would have been to know God in a way He had not yet revealed Himself.

The term "Christ," as it applies to Jesus, is an incarnational term—that is, it speaks of God as He is manifest in the flesh. Thus it is difficult to see how this verse could refer to "Christ" being identified with the people of God in the Old Testament prior to the Incarnation, unless it simply means the Spirit that later became incarnate. (For similar usage, see I Corinthians 10:4; I Peter 1:11.) In other words, Moses chose the reproach of following God, whose people would later endure similar reproach with Him when He manifested Himself in flesh.

Some commentators have suggested that since "the Christ" is equivalent to "the Anointed," the reference is to the people of God rather than to an individual.[63] They sometimes use Psalm 89:51 to support this view. Then this verse would mean Moses valued the reproach of being identified with the people of God, the nation of Israel. It is true that they were anointed of God, but the first explanation given above seems most satisfying.

Moses was able to maintain the right perspective when weighing reproach against Egypt's treasures because "he looked to the reward" (NKJV). The passage does not specify the nature of this reward, but it no doubt was the reward of obedient faith, the actual success of his efforts in freeing his oppressed brethren from Egyptian bondage.

Again, the message for the original readers of this book is clear. Though they had suffered (10:32-33) for their identification with the ultimate Messiah, Jesus Christ, they were to bear "His reproach" (13:13). Indeed, like Moses, they should esteem His reproach to be "greater riches" than the "treasures in Egypt," a not-too-veiled allusion to the law of Moses, which was still very appealing to the senses of first-century Jews, but which was obsolete (8:13). If this allusion is surprising, we should remember that Paul described the covenant established at Mount Sinai as a covenant of bondage and represented it by Hagar (Galatians 4:23-25) and that John made the earthly city of Jerusalem in the first century correspond to Sodom and Egypt (Revelation 11:8). John identified Jerusalem as the city "where also our Lord was crucified" (NKJV), tying the Jewish rejection of the Messiah, and thus their preference for the law of Moses, to their spiritual identification as Sodom and Egypt. The next verse, Hebrews 11:27, has Moses forsaking Egypt, and the purpose of Hebrews is to encourage its first readers to cling to Jesus and to forsake the law. These points further indicate that this verse uses Egypt to represent the law in making an application to its readers.

Believers must be willing to suffer discomfort on this earth, if need be, to identify with Jesus Christ. (See John 15:18-21.) They are best able to do this when they, like Moses, look "to the reward." Whatever suffering they endure now will be far overshadowed by the joys of the eternal realm. (See 12:2.)

Verse 27. Moses' rejection of his Egyptian heritage and privileges was an act of faith. The king had discovered Moses' premature attempt to introduce himself to his Hebrew brethren as their deliverer by killing the Egyptian who was brutalizing a Hebrew, and he sought to find and kill Moses. (See Exodus 2:11-15; Acts 7:24-25.) Moses fled to the land of Midian, where he spent the next forty years. (See Acts 7:29-30.) This act was one of faith because he went out of Egypt with no visible means of sustenance; he turned his back on a visible palace and a tangible support system and "endured as seeing Him who is invisible" (NKJV). This attitude is characteristic of faith. (See verse 1.)

Josephus emphasized that Moses "left the land taking no supply of food."[64] His faith in the God he could not see with the natural eye was not in vain; God arranged for Moses' path to cross that of a priest of Midian who welcomed him into his family and gave him his daughter as a wife (Exodus 2:16-22). F. F. Bruce pointed out that this verse contains a message to the original readers of this epistle, first-century Jewish Christians in danger of defection from Christ back to Judaism, "that the invisible order is the real and permanent one, and not such a visible but transient establishment as Judaism enjoyed up to A.D. 70."[65]

Several attempts have been made to reconcile the statement here that Moses did not fear the wrath of the king with the statement in Exodus 2:14 that, when his execution of the violent Egyptian was discovered, "Moses feared and said, 'Surely this thing is known!'" (NKJV). Some have denied that Moses' flight from Egypt was connected with his fear upon learning that his action was public knowledge; others have seen this reference as having to do with Moses' departure from Egypt in the Exodus rather than with his earlier departure to Midian.[66] Contextually, the latter seems an impossible resolution. The next verse, verse 28, speaks of the Passover, which makes it unlikely that the the present verse speaks of the Exodus, which occurred after the Passover. Moreover, the king's wrath seems irrelevant to the Exodus; indeed, at that time the king desired for the Israelites to vacate the land. (See Exodus 12:31-33.)

There is another possibility for reconciling the accounts, however. Though Exodus 2:14 records that "Moses feared and said, 'Surely this thing is known!'" (NKJV), nowhere does Scripture assert that Moses feared Pharaoh. It is true that Exodus 2:15 reports that when "Pharaoh heard of this matter, he sought to kill Moses" and that "Moses fled from the face of Pharaoh and dwelt in the land of Midian" (NKJV), but nothing explicitly ties Moses' flight with fear of Pharaoh. To flee from certain death in order to fulfill the call of God on one's life is no sign of fear.[67] The writer of Hebrews was certainly familiar with the Exodus account, and he did not hesitate to report that Moses did not fear the wrath of the king.

It may be that Moses' fear, rather than being directed toward Pharaoh, was directed toward his own people, the Hebrews. That is, he did not fear for his life at their hands, but he feared that they would misinterpret his actions in killing the Egyptian in such a way as to cause them to reject him as their deliverer. Stephen's interpretation of this event seems to make this a possibility. Rather than describing Moses' flight to Midian as a response to the wrath of Pharaoh, Stephen described it as a response to his rejection by the Hebrew man who was abusing his neighbor. (See Acts 7:23-29.) The nature of inspiration requires us to consider both the record of Exodus 2:15 and that of Acts 7:29 in our attempt to arrive at a complete and accurate understanding of the purpose for Moses' flight. Actually, there is no contradiction between the two. Stephen specifically declared that Moses fled at the saying of the Hebrew man; the Exodus account does not deny this. In Exodus 2:15 is a simple statement of fact: "When Pharaoh heard of this matter, he sought to kill Moses. But Moses fled from the face of Pharaoh and dwelt in the land of Midian . . ." (NKJV). If we had no other scriptural evidence, we might assume that Moses fled as a response to Pharaoh's intention to kill him, but that would be an assumption. To say that Moses "fled from the face of Pharaoh" is a Hebraism; it means that Moses fled from Pharaoh's presence. In the broadest sense, it has reference to Egypt itself. Pharaoh's presence was felt throughout Egypt since all Egypt was his domain. But the grammatical construction of Exodus 2:15 does not demand that the flight of Moses was a response to Pharaoh's wrath.

The suggestion that Moses' fear was that his Hebrew brethren would misunderstand his intentions is further supported by Stephen's declaration that "he who did his neighbor wrong pushed him [Moses] away, saying, 'Who made you a ruler and a judge over us? Do you want to kill me as you did the Egyptian yesterday?'" (Acts 7:27-28, NKJV). This Hebrew man misinterpreted Moses' intention as a desire to become a ruler and a judge over Israel. At that point, Moses' only desire was to be their deliverer (Acts 7:25). Though he would later function as a ruler and judge in conjunction with the law given at Sinai, those roles were not in view at this time. Moses apparently feared that if the Hebrews viewed him as one who wished merely to rule and judge them rather than as one who wished to deliver them, they would reject him and fail to experience the freedom God had in store for the nation.

It is understandable that the Hebrews would have interpreted Moses' action in killing the Egyptian as a claim of authority to rule. Moses was the grandson of the Pharaoh, a representative of the civil government with authority to deal with those who violated civil law. Civil government had the responsibility to carry out capital punishment against those who shed the blood of other human beings (Genesis 9:6; Romans 13:4). In Egypt, that authority resided in the royal family, of which Moses was a member. The Hebrews may very well have thought that if Moses asserted his authority in taking the life of an Egyptian, he could certainly do the same to a Hebrew. Such action would constitute a claim to be a ruler and a judge.

The fear that prompted Moses to flee Egypt was not fear for his life at the hands of Pharaoh, but fear that his people would reject him and thereby ruin his ability to deliver them. Although he could not have anticipated the manner in which God would use him to deliver the Israelites, Moses no doubt reasoned that during his absence from Egypt this event would be forgotten and he would have a fresh opportunity to deliver his people, unsullied by his past impulsiveness. In short, when he took a stand to protect his people, he was not afraid of what the king might do, but he persisted in his course of action until he indeed delivered Israel.

Verse 28. We see Moses' faith not only in his rejection of his identity as Pharaoh's daughter and his flight from Egypt, but also in keeping the Passover. (See Exodus 12.) It was an act of faith for Moses to lead the Israelites to kill a lamb, to apply its blood to the doorposts and lintels of their houses, and to prepare and eat it in the manner the Lord commanded. It was an act of faith because it was tied to an unprecedented event—the death of the firstborn of man and beast in the houses where no blood was applied—and to the anticipation of the Exodus, which was still in the realm of hope. Moses did not demand tangible proof that the firstborn would indeed die in the houses where the Passover was not observed. His faith was the confidence of things hoped for—the Exodus— and the conviction of things not seen—the death of the firstborn. (See verse 1.)

Verse 29. The example of faith now broadens to include not only Moses but all the Israelites. By faith they passed through the Red Sea as by dry land. (See Exodus 14:13-31.) This act was one of faith because it involved explicit trust in God. The sight that greeted the eyes of the Israelites as they stood on the shore of the Red Sea observing the miraculous opening of the dry passage was unprecedented. Fear and skepticism could easily have found root in their hearts if they pondered the possibility that the sea which had parted could as easily come together again, even as they attempted to cross to the other side. But their hopeful confidence in God for deliverance from Egypt and their conviction that He would deliver them, even though that deliverance was not yet finalized, enabled them to strike out across the floor of the Red Sea with walls of water towering on each side. The Egyptians, who were not people of faith, drowned attempting to cross the Red Sea. Here we see the necessity of works to accompany faith and the uselessness of works apart from faith. (See James 2:20.) The Israelites expressed their faith by crossing the sea; the attempt of the Egyptians to do the same apart from faith was futile.

10. Joshua and Israel (11:30)

(30) By faith the walls of Jericho fell down, after they were compassed about seven days.

Verse 30. The Israelite conquest of Jericho is a classic example of faith. It involved behavior that looked foolish on the surface: the men of war were to march around the city once each day for six days accompanied by seven priests bearing seven trumpets before the ark. On the seventh day, they were to march around the city seven times. The priests were to make a long blast with the trumpets, and the people were to give a great shout. Then, the Lord said, "The wall of the city will fall down flat." (See Joshua 6:1-21.) Joshua and the Israelites acted by faith because they had no tangible evidence that all this marching, trumpeting, and shouting would indeed cause the city wall to fall. There was no precedent for these actions. But, because the Lord had spoken, they were confident that the thing they hoped for—victory over Jericho—would be theirs if they were obedient. They were convinced of things not seen. (See verse 1.)

11. Rahab (11:31)

(31) By faith the harlot Rahab perished not with them that believed not, when she had received the spies with peace.

Verse 31. In the midst of the discussion of people of faith comes Rahab, an example that must have jarred Jewish believers in the first century. The first strike against Rahab was that she was not a Hebrew; she was a Gentile inhabitant of Jericho. The second strike was that she was a woman; Jewish men in the first century tended to devalue women. (See Matthew 15:23; Luke 24:10-22; John 4:27.) It is said that devout Jewish men of the time daily thanked God that he had not made them Gentiles or women. The third strike against Rahab was that she was an immoral woman, a harlot.

There could be no better way to illustrate that all people, regardless of ethnicity, gender, or social status have equal access to God on the basis of faith than to include Abraham and Rahab in the same list. The Book of James treats this subject in the same manner. (See James 2:21-25.)

Rahab demonstrated faith in Israel's God by the welcome she gave the spies into her home and her protection of them from the king of Jericho. (See Joshua 2:1-21; James 2:25.) She had heard the report of the exploits of the Lord on behalf of His people, and she confessed that Israel's God "is God in heaven above and on earth beneath." (See Joshua 2:9-11.) She was confident that the not-yet-seen thing she hoped for—the deliverance of her family from destruction when the Israelites took Jericho—would come to pass if she trusted in the God of Israel.

Rahab stands in contrast here with "those who did not believe." The lack of faith in the true God sealed the doom of most of the inhabitants of Jericho; faith in Him spared Rahab and her family. As a result of her faith, this formerly immoral Gentile woman found a place in the ancestry of the Messiah. (See Matthew 1:5-6; Luke 3:31-32.)

12. Various Heroes of Faith (11:32-40)

(32) And what shall I more say? for the time would fail me to tell of Gedeon, and of Barak, and of Samson, and of Jephthae; of David also, and Samuel, and of the prophets: (33) who through faith subdued kingdoms, wrought righteousness, obtained promises, stopped the mouths of lions, (34) quenched the violence of fire, escaped the edge of the sword, out of weakness were made strong, waxed valiant in fight, turned to flight the armies of the aliens. (35) Women received their dead raised to life again: and others were tortured, not accepting deliverance; that they might obtain a better resurrection: (36) and others

159

*had trial of cruel mockings and scourgings, yea,
moreover of bonds and imprisonment: (37) they were
stoned, they were sawn asunder, were tempted, were
slain with the sword: they wandered about in sheep-
skins and goatskins; being destitute, afflicted, tormented; (38) (of whom the world was not worthy:)
they wandered in deserts, and in mountains, and in
dens and caves of the earth. (39) And these all, having
obtained a good report through faith, received not the
promise: (40) God having provided some better thing
for us, that they without us should not be made perfect.*

Verse 32. After discussing in some detail heroes of
faith beginning with Abel and extending through Rahab,
each of whom demonstrates the nature of faith in its confidence of things hoped for and conviction of things not
seen (verse 1), it is as if the writer of Hebrews suddenly
realized that if he continued in this vein, it would con-
sume more time than he had available. And why should he
continue? The examples he had already given demonstrated his point conclusively. To continue to trace
through the Hebrew Scriptures, providing as much detail
as is given on the men and women of faith already mentioned, would be a massive task. The Hebrew Scriptures
are characterized by accounts of those who responded to
specific commands or promises of God with trusting obedience. Therefore, the author concluded his treatment of
this subject in a summary fashion, by quickly listing various additional heroes of faith—named and unnamed—
and giving a synopsis of the results of their faith.

In this section, which extends through verse 38, is a

discovery that should have been meaningful to the original readers of this letter: Though faith sometimes results in deliverance from unpleasant circumstances, there is no assurance that this will always be the case. Faith sometimes has painful consequences, including death. If the first-century Jewish Christians abandoned faith in Christ because of their sufferings (10:32-33; 12:3-4, 12, 15) and because of unrealized hopes (2:1; 3:12-14; 6:12; 10:23; 11:1), they would reject the example of their ancestors whose faith in God was unshaken by disappointment.

The first person of faith in this summary is Israel's sixth judge, Gideon, who—like all the heroes of faith before him—responded to God's initiative in such a way as to give Israel a miraculous victory over Midian. (See Judges 6:11-40; 7:1-25.) The idea to defeat Midian with a mere three hundred men armed with trumpets, pitchers and torches was certainly not Gideon's. No positive thinker was he! (See Judges 6:12-13, 15.) Even after the Lord promised Gideon that He would use him to defeat the Midianites, Gideon twice put out a fleece to confirm God's promise (Judges 6:36-40). But in the final analysis, Gideon did trust God and discovered that where there is faith one can be confident of things hoped for and convinced of things not seen. In the case of Gideon, this unseen, seemingly impossible hope was the defeat of the Midianites.

The next person of faith to appear in this summary is Barak, the fifth judge over the nation of Israel. (See Judges 4-5.) God used Barak, together with Deborah, the fourth judge, to defeat Sisera, the commander of the army of Jabin, king of Canaan. This defeat occurred in a most dramatic way, as God caused the River Kishon to flood by heavy rain, overflowing the plain where the battle was waged and miring Sisera's nine hundred iron chariots in the mud. (See Judges 4:13, 15; 5:21:22.) Every man in Sisera's army was killed by the sword except Sisera, who fled on foot (Judges 4:15-17). His escape was short-lived, however. Sisera met his death in the tent of Jael, the wife of Heber the Kenite, as she hammered a tent peg through his temple, nailing him to the earth as he slept. (See Judges 4:17-22; 5:24-27.) Again, we see faith as a human response to divine initiative: Barak's victory was the result of his obedience to God's command (Judges 4:6-10.)

The third person of faith mentioned in Hebrew's summary is Samson, the thirteenth judge of Israel, whose story is told in Judges 13-16. Although Samson frequently disobeyed the law of God, he also often acted in faith. By faith he killed a lion, thirty men of Ashkelon, a thousand Philistines, and, in his death, three thousand more Philistines (Judges 14:5-6, 19; 15:14-15; 16:27-30). He did these things as the Spirit of the Lord came upon him.

The fourth person in this summary of the heroes of faith is Jephthah, the ninth judge of Israel. (See Judges 11-12.) Jephthah was the son of Gilead by a harlot. Though his family had rejected him, the elders of Gilead later asked him to rule over them. God used him to deliver Israel from the Ammonites by a decisive victory. This victory occurred as the Spirit of the Lord came upon him (Judges 11:29); it was thus a result of his faith.

The fifth hero of faith listed by Hebrews in this concluding statement is David, the great king of Israel. Though David's life was characterized by faith, faith was nowhere more evident than in his defense of Israel against Goliath when David was still a young man. (See I Samuel 17:45-47.) We see David's faith in that he conquered Goliath "in the name of the LORD of hosts."

The last hero of faith mentioned by name is Samuel, who served as a prophet and a judge in ancient Israel. Like David, his life was characterized by faith. A shining example of Samuel's faith is the victory over the Philistines that prevailed as long as he judged Israel. (See I Samuel 7:9-17.)

At this point, Hebrews terminates its listing of people of faith by name and offers unnamed prophets as further examples of faith. Israel, of course, had many prophets. The summary that follows offers clues as to the identity of some of these prophets.

Verse 33-35a. Here, in summary fashion, we see the results of the faith of some of Israel's heroes. Some subdued kingdoms. These kingdoms included the peoples who populated the land of Canaan prior to Israel's arrival. Some people of faith worked righteousness or, as the words *ergasanto dikaiosunen* could be translated, "administered justice" (NIV). This translation seems preferred from the context with its emphasis on Israel's judges. Some obtained promises. They acted by faith to lay hold on specific promises from God. Some, like the prophet Daniel, stopped the mouths of lions. Some, like the three young Hebrew men, quenched the violence of fire. Though they were cast into the fire, it did them no violence, or harm. Some people of faith escaped the edge of the sword. This comment may refer to prophets like Elijah, upon whose life Jezebel's threat was unsuccessful. (See I Kings 19:2.) Though he perceived his own weakness, Gideon was made strong, became valiant in battle, and turned to flight the Midianite army. There is more than one account in the Hebrew Scriptures of women who received their dead raised to life again. (See I Kings 17:17-24; II Kings 4:18-37.)

A common theme runs throughout these accounts. As men and women of old believed the words of God, trusted in Him, and obeyed His commands, they received the things for which they hoped. They saw things previously invisible. (See verse 1.)

Verses 35b-38. But faith does not always result in deliverance from unpleasant circumstances. It sometimes has painful immediate consequences. No doubt this message was even more pertinent to the original readers of the book. Their experiences to this point were apparently more in harmony with those whose hopes were never realized on this earth and with those who never saw the invisible things. (See 2:1; 3:12-14; 6:12; 10:23, 32-33; 11:1; 12:3-4, 12, 15.)

Some, by faith, refused deliverance from torture in order to obtain a better resurrection. That is, they suffered for their faith rather than denying their faith in order to be spared a painful death. (See Matthew 5:10-12.) They did so in order to enjoy the resurrection to life rather than to condemnation. (See John 5:28-39; Acts 24:15; Revelation 20:13.) The Greek verb translated "tortured" (*tympanizo*) suggests the idea of being stretched on a rack and beaten to death.[68] This was the fate of Eleazar of the Maccabaean days.[69] The faith of others was tried by mockery, scourging, and unjust imprisonment. Still other people of faith were stoned, which was a common form of execution among the Jewish people. Jewish tradition declares that the prophet Isaiah was sawn in two with a wooden saw by the servants of King Manasseh.[70]

Though some people of faith escaped death by the sword (verse 34), others were slain by the sword.[71] There were those whose faith resulted in homelessness as they wandered about, destitute, afflicted, tormented, clothed in the skins of sheep and goats.

Though these people of faith had little standing in the social community—they wandered the deserts and mountains, making their homes in caves and holes in the earth—their faith set them apart so radically from unbelievers that the world was unworthy of them. Their lives were characterized by a focus on invisible hopes rather than material possessions, but they were people of character.

The point is well made: our greatest opportunity and responsibility is to trust God, whether that trust results in joyous deliverance from painful circumstances or whether it has unpleasant results and its promises are never realized on this earth. The first readers of this letter would be more likely to identify with the latter, but the example of their ancestors should have served to encourage them to keep their faith in Jesus Christ regardless of their temporal disappointments.

Verse 39. All the heroes of faith mentioned by name or left unidentified in this chapter "obtained a good testimony through faith" (NKJV). This is true regardless of whether their faith had pleasant or unpleasant temporal consequences. (See verses 32-38.) This verse echoes the sentiments of verses 2 and 13: on the basis of faith a person obtains a good testimony, and even if death precedes the fulfillment of a promise, it is no indication that the person who died before receiving a promise lacked faith.

165

That these people of faith "obtained a good testimony" means we can witness, even as in this chapter, that their faith in God was genuine. But beyond that, the phrase implies that they were justified, or gained right standing with God, on the basis of their faith. (See comments on verse 2 and Romans 4:3.)

But even though the examples in this chapter were people of unquestionable faith, they "did not receive the promise" (NKJV). Verse 33 points out that some "obtained promises," and verse 13 reveals that some died without receiving the promises, but the promises in view in those verses are distinct from *the* promise addressed here. God gave various individuals discussed in this chapter many promises. Some were fulfilled during the lifetimes of the people to whom they were given; others were not. (See verse 13.) But the ultimate promise, which involved the coming of the Messiah, the new covenant, and the outpouring of the Holy Spirit, was not fulfilled during the lifetimes of any of the people of faith mentioned in this chapter. (See comments on 9:15; 10:36.)

Jesus specifically identified the promise of the Father as the baptism with the Holy Spirit (Acts 1:4-5). This statement ties the baptism with the Holy Spirit to the promises of the Hebrew prophets that a new era was coming which would be characterized by an unprecedented work of the Holy Spirit in the lives of God's people. (See Isaiah 59:20-21; Jeremiah 31:31-34; Ezekiel 36:25-27; 37:14; 39:29; Joel 2:28-29; John 7:37-39.) Although this promise awaits its final fulfillment as it pertains to national Israel (Romans 11:12, 26-27), it is enjoyed at this time in the church, where ethnic origins are of no significance. (See Acts 2:16-21, 33, 38-39; Galatians 3:28; Colossians 3:11.)

Verse 40. The "something better" that God has provided for us is "the promise" of verse 39. Regardless of the
inspiring heroics of the people of faith and the rewards
received by those whose faith had pleasant consequences—including translation (verse 5), miraculous
preservation of life during the worldwide flood (verse 7),
miraculous conception (verse 11), miraculous provision
(verses 17-19), miraculous protection (verse 23, 28, 31,
33), miraculous deliverance (verse 29, 34), miraculous
victory (verse 30, 34), and resurrection from the dead
(verse 35)—the provisions of the new covenant are far
better. The glory of the new covenant causes everything
before it to pale by comparison. Indeed, all that preceded
the coming of Christ was merely a shadow of Him. (See
10:1; Colossians 2:16-17; Luke 24:27, 44-45; John 5:39.)
The new covenant is superior to all covenants before it
because it is based on better promises. (See comments on
8:6.)

In view of the miraculous experiences of many people
of faith in the pre-Messianic era, how can we say that we
now have "something better"? The new covenant is better because it involves the Incarnation, wherein God
Himself walks among people (John 1:1, 14; I Timothy
3:16; I John 1:1-2), the permanent forgiveness of sin
based on the Atonement (8:12-13; 9:26; 10:4, 10, 17),
life in the Spirit rather than by the letter of the law (Galatians 3:2-5; II Corinthians 3:6-11), and the promise of
eternal life rather than merely long life in the earthly land
of promise (see 9:15; I John 2:25).

As great as were the experiences of many people of
faith before the coming of Christ, the inferiority of the
covenants under which they lived and the incompleteness

of the revelation they received means that "they should not be made perfect apart from us" (NKJV). This comment indicates the solidarity of people of faith on both sides of the Cross. The point is that God has only one basis upon which people are "made perfect" (Greek, *teleiothosin*, which has to do with being brought to the end or purpose of a thing), and that is the Cross. (See 10:14; 12:23.) Whether a person of faith lived and died before the coming of Jesus or whether he lives in the present era, it is by the Cross that he or she receives "perfection" (which, in the ultimate sense, is salvation). Though the vision of those who lived prior to the Cross could not have been as clear as we now enjoy, it is faith and not the extent of the revelation received that procures the benefits of the Cross. (See 10:36.) If people of faith before the coming of Christ had realized the ultimate fulfillment of their hopes—or had been "made perfect"—apart from those who lived in the Messianic era, it would mean that God had more than one means of providing redemption. It would mean that the Cross of Christ, rather than being the unique means of dealing with sins, would merely be *a* means. But God has no other basis upon which to cleanse people from sin (10:4). The blood of Jesus is His exclusive provision for redemption (10:19-20).

The message chapter 11 communicated to the original readers of Hebrews is this: Though the faith of those who lived prior to the coming of Christ was genuine, and though it often resulted in miracles—but often it simply gave faithful people the ability to endure hardship—the experience of all those mentioned was inferior to the experience of participants in the new covenant. Those in the pre-Messianic era "did not receive *the* promise" (verse

39); what God has provided for us is better. This fact should have convinced the original readers to abandon any thought of defecting from Christ and His new covenant to return to a covenant always inferior and now outmoded. (See 8:6-13; 10:1-5, 8-9, 26-29, 35-39; 12:18-24.)

III.

God Disciplines His Children
(12:1-29)

A. Follow the Example of Jesus
(12:1-4)

(1) Wherefore seeing we also are compassed about with so great a cloud of witnesses, let us lay aside every weight, and the sin which doth so easily beset us, and let us run with patience the race that is set before us, (2) looking unto Jesus the author and finisher of our faith; who for the joy that was set before him endured the cross, despising the shame, and is set down at the right hand of the throne of God. (3) For consider him that endured such contradiction of sinners against himself, lest ye be wearied and faint in your minds. (4) Ye have not yet resisted unto blood, striving against sin.

This section of the letter provides insight as to why the first readers were tempted to turn away from Christ and the new covenant to return to the law of Moses: They had mistaken God's chastening for abandonment (verses 5-8). They interpreted the pain and discomfort accompanying divine discipline to mean they had made the wrong decision in believing on Jesus. Like the ancient Israelites who looked back to life in Egypt with nostalgic yearning (Exodus 14:11-12; 16:2-3; 17:3), these first-century Jewish believers fondly recalled their life under the law, forgetting their lack of intimacy with God (verses 18-21), the inability of the law to bring them to maturity (7:18-19), and their inability to obey the law's impossible demands (Romans 8:3). (See Acts 15:10; Galatians 3:10-12; 4:9.)

The focus of Hebrews to this point has been to assure the original readers that they did not do the wrong thing to believe on Jesus and that their suffering was not unprecedented for people of faith. Instead of responding to suffering by turning away from Jesus, they needed to respond by recognizing the loving hand of their heavenly Father in their difficulty. His chastening was for their long-term benefit (verses 11-17).

Verse 1. Believers are surrounded by a great "cloud of witnesses." These "witnesses" are those who have gone before who have stood fast in their faith regardless of the circumstances of life. Specifically, these witnesses include all those mentioned in Hebrews 11 who "obtained a good testimony through faith" (11:39). The example of these witnesses should encourage believers in this era to deal decisively with distractions by laying them aside and to endure until they receive faith's ultimate reward.

This verse draws a vivid word picture. The word translated "cloud" (Greek, *nephos*) describes a vast cloud mass, and the metaphor "refers to the great amphitheatre with the arena for the runners and the tiers upon tiers of seats rising up like a cloud."[72] The people of faith from the previous era are not merely spectators observing the agonizing struggles of believers in the present era; they have been through the same struggles themselves. The picture the author had in mind may be something like that of "a relay race where those who have finished their course and handed in their baton are watching and encouraging their successors."[73]

In view of the example of those who ran before them, believers are to "lay aside every weight." The word translated "lay aside" (Greek, *apothemenoi*) also appears in Colossians 3:8, which commands believers to "put off" sinful behavior. The word has to do with laying off old clothing.[74] The word translated "weight" (Greek, *ogkon*) describes any handicapping encumbrance. The idea is that in a race, there should be no "trailing garment to hinder or trip" the runner.[75] This statement is similar to the descriptions elsewhere of people "girding up their loins" to run (II Kings 4:29; 9:1) and of believers "girding up the loins of their minds" (I Peter 1:13). Since the long, flowing garments worn at that time could easily hamper and trip a runner, it was necessary to tuck the tail of the garment into the sash ("girdle"). Here, however, the believer is not simply advised to "gird up his loins," but to lay aside every hindrance to the race of faith. In ancient Rome, runners in the stadium raced naked or nearly naked.[76] Since the verse goes on to urge the laying aside of sin as well, it may be that the weights are not inherently sinful. They are, however, hindrances to endurance.

For the original readers of this letter, these weights may have included a failure to engage daily in mutual encouragement (3:13; 10:24), a lack of diligence in entering into Christ's rest by ceasing to depend upon one's own works to gain merit with God (4:10-11), a lack of boldness in approaching the throne of grace (4:16), an immature fascination with the elementary principles of Christ and a failure to go on to the solid food (5:12-14; 6:1), a sluggishness in faith and patience (6:12), and a failure to assemble faithfully with believers for mutual exhortation (10:25). For believers at other times and places, hindrances that they need to lay aside may include these or other things which, though not necessarily inherently sinful, prevent them from doing their best in the Christian race. It is so important for us to finish the race successfully that the appeal to lay aside even non-sinful hindrances is justified. The carrying of unnecessary weights, even if they are not sinful, may make us more susceptible to sin itself.

Not only are believers to lay aside weights, they are to lay aside "the sin which so easily ensnares." For the original readers of this letter, this sin included "an evil heart of unbelief in departing from the living God" (3:12), apostasy (the rejection of previously revealed truths and valid spiritual experiences) (6:6), a rejection of Jesus Christ and His atoning work (10:26-31), and a rejection of the life of faith (10:38-39). These specific sins could easily ensnare the first recipients of this letter because, as Jews, they had lived their lives under the law of Moses, a covenant given for a radically different purpose than the new covenant. Though the law was valid, it had been widely abused by the Hebrew people, who viewed it as an end in itself and who sought to gain right standing with God on the basis of the works of the law (Romans 9:31-32). This erroneous perspective was so deeply ingrained in the minds of the Jewish people that they struggled mightily with the idea that they could attain right standing with God only by faith in Jesus Christ. They had a deep-seated and time-honored belief that the law was the ultimate and final revelation of God. Jewish tradition claimed that when the Messiah came, the writings of the prophets and the poetic books would be abrogated, but not the law.[77] Since only a small minority of Jewish people had placed their faith in Jesus Christ, they were constantly exposed to the temptation to return to the law, which arose from the influence of unbelieving family and friends. In such an environment, it was relatively easily to defect from the new covenant back to the law.

For believers today, other sins may easily ensnare. In many cases, these kinds of sins may be those associated with our life before coming to Christ, just as the law was associated with the first readers of this letter in the days before their faith in Christ. For this reason, each person must make a careful, prayerful, and realistic assessment of himself to determine what kind of decisions he should make so as to enhance his potential for successful completion of the Christian race and to decrease his potential for defeat. It may be necessary for some to lay aside behaviors in which others can engage. Something that is a weight and could easily develop into a sin for one person may not be a hindrance to another. (See Romans 14.)

The reason believers are to lay aside hindering weights and easily ensnaring sins is so we can "run with endurance the race that is set before us." The race in view is not a short sprint but a long-distance run that requires endurance and persistence.[78] The word translated "race" is *agona*, from which the English "agony" is derived and a form of which is translated "striving" in verse 4. Here, the Christian life is described as a race requiring intense effort and even pain. Athletic symbolism is not uncommon in the

New Testament. (See I Corinthians 9:24, 26; Galatians 2:2; 5:7; Philippians 2:16; I Timothy 6:12; II Timothy 4:7.)

Verse 2. As the believer runs the Christian race, he is to look steadfastly "unto Jesus, the author and finisher of our faith." The first readers of this letter were tempted to look away from Jesus and back to the law. (See 2:1-3; 3:1, 12; 6:6; 10:29, 39.) Instead, the author urged them not to be distracted by various hindrances and sins (verse 1); they should keep their gaze fastened unswervingly on Jesus. Just as a runner keeps his eyes on the finish line— his ultimate goal—so the believer must hold Jesus as the final goal of his life.

The word translated "author" (Greek, *archegon*) appears also in 2:10, where it is translated "captain." "Finisher" is translated from *teleioten*, a word the writer of Hebrews apparently coined from *teleioo*, for it has not been found elsewhere.[79] *Teleioo* has to do with completion, maturity, or consummation. The word "our" does not appear in the Greek text. The point seems to be that Jesus is the originator and completer of faith. To the first readers of Hebrews, this description meant that the same Jesus who first caused faith to arise in their hearts would, if they looked only to Him, complete what He started. (See Philippians 1:6.)

The struggles of the Jewish believers to whom this letter was first addressed were not unknown to Jesus. They were experiencing sufferings, reproaches, and tribulations (10:32-33); He had endured the shameful death of the cross. Though He despised the shame associated with death on a cross (Deuteronomy 21:23; Galatians 3:13; Matthew 26:39-42; Philippians 2:8), He nevertheless endured it "for the joy that was set before Him." A consideration of the reward for endurance of the pain made the suffering bearable. Likewise, if believers keep in mind the ultimate reward of faith, they can endure persecution and other uncomfortable circumstances.

The joy that was set before Jesus was the knowledge that by His suffering He would provide redemption for the world. (See Matthew 18:11.)

The word translated "has sat down" (Greek, *kekathiken*) is in the perfect tense, which indicates not only that He sat down at some point in the past but that He remains seated. (On "the right hand of the throne of God," see the discussion on "the right hand of the Majesty on high" in 1:3.)

Verse 3. In chapter 11, the writer of Hebrews held up for the consideration of his readers the heroes of faith from Abel to unnamed sufferers and martyrs. These people lived by faith in spite of their failure to receive faith's ultimate reward. (See 11:39.) These examples, drawn from the ranks of human beings who stood in solidarity with the first readers of this letter, should have encouraged the first Jewish audience to divest themselves of distracting hindrances, whether or not they were sinful, in order to be able to endure patiently to the end of the race. (See verse 1.) But the ultimate example is Jesus Christ Himself. (See verse 2.) No one had suffered more significantly than He, though no one deserved it less. In spite of the shame associated with death on a cross, Jesus had been able to endure it by focusing on the ultimate joy that would result from His suffering.

For this reason verse 3 urges believers to "consider Him who endured such hostility from sinners against Himself." The first readers of this letter were not the only ones who had ever suffered for their faith. Because it is easy to "become weary and discouraged in your souls" (NKJV) when we think we are alone in our sufferings, or if we think our sufferings are unprecedented, we should remind ourselves of others whose sufferings were perhaps even greater. (See Matthew 5:10-12.) The One whose sufferings were most intense—due to His complete innocence and the vicarious nature of His sufferings—is Jesus Christ. Peter considered the example of Christ's wrongful sufferings to be instructive for all believers. (See I Peter 2:19-23.)

The hostility that Jesus endured was "against Himself." Strictly speaking, the persecution believers experience is not directed against them; it is due to their identification with Jesus Christ. (See I Peter 4:16.) Thus, believers do not experience personal rejection, as did Jesus. This fact helps put into perspective the persecution associated with being identified with Christ.

God created human beings to exist in a social context; it is not good that man be alone. (See Genesis 2:18.) The first social context in which a person exists is the family. Thus, it is especially devastating to be rejected by one's family. But it is sometimes the consequence of identification with Jesus Christ. (See Matthew 10:21, 34-36.) Being rejected by one's family can result in great mental and spiritual weariness and discouragement. Remembering that this kind of rejection is not due to one's personal lack of worth but rather due to enmity against Jesus Christ can help a person retain his spiritual strength and courage.

The word translated "consider" (Greek, *analogisasthe*) occurs only here in the New Testament, and it "conveys the idea of comparison as well as considering."[80] We are not only to consider the sufferings of Jesus; we are to compare them with our own. When we do so, our sufferings fall into perspective. Jesus is the only one ever to suffer who was completely innocent. (See Isaiah 53:4-5, 8-12.) He is also the only one whose sufferings were vicarious. (See I Peter 2:24.)

Verse 4. The comparison urged upon the original readers of this letter would reveal that they had not yet suffered to the same degree as Jesus. He had been crucified; they had "not yet resisted to bloodshed." Their suffering was real (see 10:32-33), but it was not as intense as what Jesus or other believers had experienced. (See II Corinthians 6:4-5; 11:23-27.) Jesus had "endured . . . hostility from sinners against Himself"; the first readers of this letter had been "striving against sin" itself (NKJV). Peter addressed the same issue: "Therefore, since Christ suffered for us in the flesh, arm yourselves also with the same mind, for he who has suffered in the flesh has ceased from sin" (I Peter 4:1, NKJV).

There is a certain suffering associated with denying sinful impulses. The natural tendency of the flesh is toward sin; to deny the flesh its sinful indulgence is to put it to death. (See Romans 6:11-13.) Believers are positionally identified with Jesus Christ in His death; they are to live out this identification by resisting temptation. (See Romans 6:2-6.) This process is painful because it involves the moment-by-moment, day-by-day yielding of one's members—body, soul and spirit—to the leading of the Holy Spirit rather than to the impulses of sin. (See Romans 6:13-19.) Though the Holy Spirit works within the believer to give right desires and abilities (Philippians

2:13), the sin principle is also still there, struggling against the Spirit. (See Galatians 5:16-17.) There is suffering here, but it is nothing compared to the sufferings Jesus Christ endured.

The specific sin against which the original readers of this letter struggled was apostasy. Because of their past associations, ongoing rejection by their non-Messianic Jewish brethren, and the apparent continuing prosperity of Temple worship, they were tempted to renounce their faith in Christ and to turn back to the law.

Alternatively, the struggle against sin to which this verse refers may be the enmity of those who rejected Christ. In other words, the first readers of this letter had to struggle against those who attempted to persuade them to abandon their faith in Jesus. Both the word "striving" here and "race" in verse 1 are translated from a form of the Greek *agona*, from which we derive the English "agony." The word underscores the effort and pain associated with resisting temptations to abandon the Christian life and to endure to the end.

That the first readers of this letter had "not yet resisted to bloodshed" may help narrow the range of possible recipients and dates for the writing of the letter.[81] (See comments on 10:32-33.)

B.

Those Who Are Chastened
Are God's Sons
(12:5-11)

(5) And ye have forgotten the exhortation which speaketh unto you as unto children, My son, despise not thou the chastening of the Lord, nor faint when thou art rebuked of him: (6) for whom the Lord loveth he chasteneth, and scourgeth every son whom he receiveth. (7) If ye endure chastening, God dealeth with you as with sons; for what son is he whom the father chasteneth not? (8) But if ye be without chastisement, whereof all are partakers, then are ye bastards, and not sons. (9) Furthermore we have had fathers of our flesh which corrected us, and we gave them reverence: shall we not much rather be in subjection unto the Father of spirits, and live? (10) For they verily for a few days chastened us after their own pleasure; but he for our profit, that we might be partakers of his holiness. (11) Now no chastening for the present seemeth to be joyous, but grievous: nevertheless afterward it yieldeth the peaceable fruit of righteousness unto them which are exercised thereby.

Verses 5-6. One of the reasons the original readers of this letter were tempted to turn away from Christ was that they had confused God's discipline with abandonment.

(See comments before 12:1.) They had "forgotten the exhortation which [spoke to them] as to sons." The exhortation in view is in Proverbs 3:11-12. As elsewhere, Hebrews quotes the Septuagint translation.

When we forget biblical principles, we are always in danger of losing our faith. One of the first consequences of forgetfulness is misjudging God. If we do not know how or why God acts as He does, we may think He is unconcerned or unjust. We may even question His omniscience, omnipotence, omnipresence, or existence. Although we will never have the answers to all possible questions in this life, unanswered questions should drive us back to the Bible rather than cause us to lose faith in God. It may be that we have misunderstood some biblical teaching.

The exhortation of Proverbs 3:11-12 speaks to those who are sons of God, not to those who have never known Him. The painful circumstances in the lives of unbelievers may have different causes, but it is always possible that the believer's discomfort is due to divine discipline.

Believers are not to despise the chastening of the Lord. The word "despise" (Greek, *oligorei*) means we are not to "make light of" His chastening. Children are sometimes tempted to reject the discipline of their human parents as pointless and meaningless. But discipline that is rejected bears no positive fruit. (See verse 11.) Those who despise the chastening of the Lord may find His continuing chastening to be even more painful. (See I Corinthians 11:30-32.)

The Lord does not intend His rebuke to cause discouragement. If we remember the Lord's motive in chastening (verses 10, 14), His rebuke will be cause for rejoicing, for it is evidence that He still loves us, considers us His children, and has hope for our future. The truly frightening thought would not be the chastening of a loving heavenly Father, but to think that He has given up on us. (See Romans 1:24, 26, 28; I John 5:16.)

Verses 7-8. In his own words rather than those of Proverbs 3:11-12, the writer of Hebrews reiterated that chastening is evidence that God is dealing with us as sons. Chastening is inherent in the father-son relationship. The only people whom God does not chasten are those who are not His sons. That they are illegitimate means that they do not have God for their father. (See John 8:42-44.)

Although it may not have lessened their pain, this discussion of divine discipline should have encouraged the original readers of Hebrews. Having forgotten the message of Proverbs 3:11-12, they were in danger of misinterpreting the circumstances of life. It should have brought them hope to know that they were still the sons of God and that He was actively involved with all the events of their lives, even the painful ones.

Verse 9. It should come as no surprise that our heavenly Father disciplines us. Even in the human realm, we experience discipline. In addition to its advice on response to the chastening of the Lord, the Book of Proverbs addresses the role of chastening in rearing children. (See Proverbs 13:24; 19:18; 22:15; 23:13-14; 29:15.) If we are wise children, our response to the correction of our human fathers is to pay them respect. If we are willing to respond in this way to correction on a purely human level, "shall we not much more readily be in subjection to the Father of spirits and live?" (NKJV) We should be even more willing to respond in a positive way to God's chastening than we are to acknowledge the legitimacy of the discipline given by our human fathers. The result of proper response to God's chastening is life.

The precise phrase "Father of spirits" appears nowhere else in Scripture. The phrase "God of the spirits of all flesh" appears in Numbers 16:22; 27:16. In the context of Hebrews, we should not suppose that the writer intended to communicate specific insight concerning the makeup of the immaterial part of humans. He did not mean that God is the Father of the human spirit only and is not related to any other aspect of human existence. Rather, the contrast is between human fathers and our heavenly Father. The phrase "human fathers" in the NKJV is *tes sarkos hemon pateras*, which literally translates as "fathers of our flesh." This phrase stands in obvious contrast to *toi patri ton pneumaton*, "to the Father of spirits."

The purpose of the verse, then, is not to establish an anthropology (doctrine of humanity). It does not mean that children derive only their physical body from their parents but derive their spirit from God. The anthropological view that seems most satisfying biblically is traducianism, which teaches that a person receives all his existence, material and immaterial, from his parents.[82]

The life that results from proper response to the chastening of the Lord is eternal life, whereas proper response to the discipline of human fathers tended to result in long life on this earth. (See Exodus 20:12; Ephesians 6:2-3.) We know the life promised as a result of subjection to the Father of spirits is eternal life because His discipline is designed to bring us to share in His holiness (verse 10), and without this holiness "no one will see the Lord" (verse 14, NKJV).

Verse 10. The discipline our human fathers gave us was "for a few days." That is, it extended only as long as we were under their authority. We are always obliged to honor our parents (Exodus 20:12; Deuteronomy 5:16), but we are obliged to obey them only so long as we are "children" still in the process of being brought up by our parents "in the Lord" (Ephesians 6:1, 4). The possibility exists that non-Christian parents may attempt to influence their children to disobey God; Christian children cannot obey such commands. (See Matthew 10:21, 34-36; Acts 5:29.) Even in a circumstance like this, however, a child must honor and respect his parents.

But whereas parental discipline terminates when a son or daughter leaves father and mother to establish a new family (Genesis 2:24), God's discipline of His children extends as far as needed.[83] Human fathers chasten their children as seems best to them; since human beings are fallible, it is always possible they could be wrong in their application of discipline. But God makes no mistakes; His chastening is always "for our profit." Specifically, the intent of His chastening is "that we may be partakers of His holiness" (NKJV).

Holiness, which has its origins in the Hebrew *qadosh*, means "separation" of some kind, with this separation being *unto* something or someone and consequently a separation *from* something or someone.[84] In this context, it is separation unto God and consequently from all that is unlike Him. Specifically, this passage identifies holiness as "the peaceable fruit of righteousness" (verse 11, 14) and the avoidance of bitterness (verse 15), sexual immorality, and profanity (verse 16).

People can be holy only as they are "partakers of His

holiness." God alone is inherently holy (Leviticus 11:44; 19:2; I Peter 1:16). Morality is not holiness, although those who are holy will be moral. Modesty is not holiness, although those who are holy will be modest. Honesty is not holiness, although those who are holy will be honest. It is possible to be relatively moral, modest, honest, and to have other positive character traits and yet to have no faith in the true God and no relationship with Him. Although those who are holy will be people of high character, it is possible to be of sterling character and to be unholy due to lack of faith in God. Biblical holiness comes only when we identify with the true God by faith in Him, and it is perfected in us as we respond to His chastening in obedience.

Verse 11. The chastening of the Lord is painful. It does not immediately promote a joyous response. Such chastening may include weakness, sickness, and premature death. (See I Corinthians 11:30-32; James 5:16.) But divine discipline to which we correctly respond ultimately "yields the peaceable fruit of righteousness to those who have been trained by it." There is a clear parallel between the "holiness" of verse 10 and "the peaceable fruit of righteousness." Both are the results of divine discipline. In other words, the holiness in view *is* the peaceable fruit of righteousness. There is a parallel between the holiness that is "the peaceable fruit of righteousness" and the command to "pursue peace with all people, and holiness" (verse 14, NJKV).

"Righteousness" is a theological term that for some people may obscure the meaning of the Greek *dikaiosunes*. The English word "righteousness" springs from the Old English "rightwiseness." It simply has to do with being right.[85] In this case, it means doing the right thing in God's eyes. This right thing is to pursue peace with all people (verse 14).

Chastening is seen here as training. The Greek *gegymnasmenois*, from which comes the English "gymnasium," is translated "trained" ("exercised," KJV). The idea, drawn from the metaphor of athletics, is that of long-term, disciplined training rather than sporadic bursts of exercise. When a believer commits himself as a way of life to responding obediently to the chastening of the Lord, permanent growth in character results. Such a result cannot come from short-term efforts.

C.

Proper Response to God's Chastening (12:12-17)

(12) Wherefore lift up the hands which hang down, and the feeble knees; (13) and make straight paths for your feet, lest that which is lame be turned out of the way; but let it rather be healed. (14) Follow peace with all men, and holiness, without which no man shall see the Lord: (15) looking diligently lest any man fail of the grace of God; lest any root of bitterness springing up trouble you, and thereby many be defiled; (16) lest there be any fornicator, or profane person, as Esau, who for one morsel of meat sold his birthright. (17) For ye know how that afterward, when he would have inherited the blessing, he was rejected: for he found no place of repentance, though he sought it carefully with tears.

Verses 12-13. Since the chastening of the Lord is a sign that those He chastens are still His children (verses 5-7) and since He intends for the chastening to profit believers, enabling them to partake of His holiness (verse 10), believers should respond by gaining new courage and repairing the paths in which they walk. "Therefore" (Greek, *dio*) refers to what has gone before.

Verse 12 closely follows the wording of Isaiah 35:3,

and verse 13 seems to borrow from Proverbs 4:26. "Hands which hang down" are limp and ineffective hands. The reference may even be to paralysis. "Feeble knees" are weak and incapable of sustained exertion in walking or standing. In the larger context of the book, the reference to the spiritual weakness of the original readers is obvious. They have become dull of hearing, and they have regressed to become babes who need milk rather than solid food (5:11-13). Hebrews 5:14 uses the Greek *gegymnasmena* to point out that only those who have their senses "exercised" to discern both good and evil are qualified for solid food. Thus the "exercise" of 5:14 is semantically related to the "training" of 12:11.

The spiritual weakness of the original readers is a consequence of walking on crooked paths. The context of the letter suggests that this crookedness results from a lack of exclusive and unswerving commitment to Jesus Christ and the new covenant. (See 6:4-6; 10:23-29, 35, 38-39.) Although they had been spiritually enlightened, tasted the heavenly gift, become partakers of the Holy Spirit, and tasted the good Word of God and the powers of the age to come (6:4-6), they were contemplating turning away from Christ and reverting to the old covenant (2:1-4). Their spiritual ambivalence caused them to be spiritually lame and in need of healing. In order to make their paths straight once again and to regain their strength, they needed to recognize the chastening hand of their loving heavenly Father in their pain, they needed to turn away decisively and permanently from the rituals of the law of Moses, and they needed to commit themselves unequivocally and exclusively to Jesus Christ.

Verse 14. To be a partaker of God's holiness is not

merely an ethereal concept. It involves purposeful conformity of one's actions to the character of God. Here, holiness is expressed in the pursuit of peace with all people. (See verse 10.) Rather than identifying the pursuit of peace and the pursuit of holiness as two different things, the context strongly links them together. (See verses 10-11.) The use of *kai* ("and") here seems to be ascensive at the least,[86] with the idea being, "Pursue peace with all people, even holiness. . . ." It may even be emphatic, with the thought being, "Pursue peace . . . indeed, pursue holiness." The adjective "which" (Greek, *ou*) is singular, apparently applying to the pursuit of both peace and holiness as a singular referent. That is, no one will see the Lord whose holiness is not characterized by the pursuit of peace with all people. Paul gave similar advice in Romans 12:18, and Jesus said peacemakers shall be called the sons of God (Matthew 5:9).

If the pursuit of peace and holiness are two different issues in this verse, then the statement "without which no one will see the Lord" can refer only to one of them, and it would apparently refer to that closest in the text, the pursuit of holiness. If we remember, however, that the problem this chapter addresses is the failure of the original readers to understand that their painful experiences were due to God's chastening, we can see the connection between the pursuit of peace with all people and holiness. If they did not recognize God's chastening hand in their pain, they would no doubt have identified those who persecuted them as their personal enemies. This attitude would have led to tensions between them and their persecutors. Thus, their recovery of holiness upon recognizing the chastening of the Lord should also have resulted in the development of peace with those they formerly perceived to be enemies. People were not their enemies; they had been instruments in the hand of God to chasten His children. Thus, the pursuit of peace with all people and the pursuit of holiness are one and the same. Those who reject the chastening of the Lord and who thus do not partake of His holiness—and who, by implication, perceive people to be their enemies—can have no expectation of seeing the Lord.

Verse 15. In addition to pursuing peace with all people, the writer of Hebrews urged his original audience to carefully avoid falling short of the grace of God. There are eight references to the grace of God in the thirteen chapters of Hebrews. The substitutionary death of Christ was a work of God's grace (2:9). The throne of God, to which believers can boldly come on the basis of Christ's high priestly work, is a throne of grace where those who come receive mercy and grace (4:16). To turn away from Christ and the new covenant is to insult the Spirit of grace (10:29). On the basis of grace, acceptable service to God is possible (12:28). By grace the heart is established so as to avoid strange doctrines (13:9). And the author's final wish for his readers is for grace to be with them (13:25).

Hebrews connects grace with the work of Christ in establishing the new covenant. To "fall short of the grace of God" is thus to turn away from Christ and the covenant He established in His blood. The original readers were in danger of doing this if they defected to the law of Moses. If they thereby failed God's grace, the result would be the springing up of a troubling bitter root that would defile many. Grammatically, the phrase "root of bitterness" refers not to bitterness itself as the troubling root, but to a root of trouble that is bitter.

The verses remaining in this chapter reveal that this bitter root would result from rejecting the new covenant like Esau rejected his birthright (verse 16). If they did this, they would discover that they had rejected their only hope to inherit God's blessing (verse 17). Just as there was no hope for Esau apart from his birthright, there is no hope for Israel apart from Jesus Christ and the new covenant. If they traded the grace of God as expressed in the new covenant for the works system of the law of Moses, an outmoded covenant (8:13), they would, like Esau, discover it to be a bitter root that would trouble and defile many. This defilement would pollute their faith and cause them to refuse the voice of God (verse 25).

Verse 16. The warning to respond correctly to the chastening of the Lord was intended to help the readers avoid the consequences of misinterpreting their circumstances. (See comments before verse 1.) These consequences would have included an inability to see the Lord (verse 14), a falling short of the grace of God, and the springing up of a troubling, bitter root that would defile the faith of many (verse 15). These would be among the consequences of those who, like Esau, undervalued their birthright. If these first-century Jewish believers turned away from Christ and the new covenant in favor of the rituals of the law of Moses, they would be guilty of the same sin as Esau, "who for one morsel of food sold his birthright" (NKJV).

There are striking parallels between Esau's failure and the potential failure of the original readers of Hebrews. Esau made the wrong decision because of his weariness and hunger (Genesis 25:29-32). He was so overwhelmed by his circumstances that he said, "I am about to die; so what is this birthright to me?" (Genesis 25:32, NKJV). Esau traded something of eternal value for momentary gratification. The Jewish believers to whom Hebrews was first written were in danger of becoming "weary and discouraged" in their souls (verse 3). Although they had not experienced martyrdom, they had been struggling against sin with the sufferings that accompany this struggle (verse 4; see also 10:32-33). If they turned away from Jesus for whatever momentary relief this action may have brought, they would have, so to speak, sold their "birthright," their claim on the Messiah and the new covenant established in His blood, for "one morsel of food," the temporary comfort of the law of Moses. If they did so, they would, like Esau, be "fornicators" and "profane" persons.

It is doubtful in this context whether the word "fornicator" has to do with physical sexual immorality. Instead, it seems to be a reference to the spiritual fornication of unfaithfulness to God. The word is used this way in a number of contexts. (See Judges 2:17; II Chronicles 21:11; Isaiah 23:17; Ezekiel 16:26, 29; Revelation 2:20; 17:2, 4; 18:3, 9; 19:2.) To turn away from the true God is to commit spiritual fornication just as a man or woman who is unfaithful to his or her spouse commits physical fornication. Here we see the exclusive nature of the new covenant; there can be no blending of the old covenant and the new. Romans 7:1-4 expresses the same idea.

Another parallel between Esau's failure and the potential failure of the original readers of this letter is that the words translated "birthright" (Greek, *prototokia*) here in verse 16 and "firstborn" (Greek, *prototokon*) in verse 23 are both from *prototokos*. Although Esau's was a natural birthright whereas theirs was a spiritual one, the first-century Jewish Christians were in danger of losing their birthright just as he had lost his. (See verse 23.)

To be "profane" (Greek, *bebelos*) is to lack spiritual values.[87] The Septuagint translation of Ezekiel 21:25 applies the word to Zedekiah due to his failure to keep his oath with the king of Babylon.[88] Zedekiah's punishment was to lose his right to the throne of David. Thus, his "profanity" had the same consequence as that of Esau: they both lost what was rightfully theirs. For Jewish believers to defect from faith in Jesus Christ would likewise be an act of profanity that would result in the loss of spiritual privileges.

Verse 17. It was impossible for Esau to recover the blessing he lost by despising his birthright. The episode in Esau's life to which this verse refers appears in Genesis 27:30-37. By deceit, Jacob obtained the blessing Isaac intended for Esau. Although Esau "cried with an exceedingly great and bitter cry, and said to his father, 'Bless me—me also, O my father!'" (Genesis 27:34, NKJV), he could not retrieve the blessing already given to Jacob. The warning for the first readers of this book was that if they rejected Christ and the new covenant, they would find themselves excluded from the blessing of God. No blessing remained in the rituals of the old covenant.

Although Hebrews compares the sale of Esau's birthright for food to the danger of apostasy, it is doubtful if we should understand the phrase "for he found no place for repentance" to mean it is absolutely impossible under any circumstances for those who have turned away from faith in Christ to recognize their error and return to Him.

(See comments on 6:6; 10:26-29.)

First, nowhere does this verse proclaim this point. The reference is simply to an episode in the life of Esau and its consequences.

Second, the nature of the birthright was that only one son could possess it. It had already been given to Jacob; therefore it could not be given to Esau. This is not the nature of the new covenant. Its blessings are not limited to one person only. Jesus said, "The one who comes to me I will by no means cast out" (John 6:37, NKJV). God is "not willing that any should perish but that all should come to repentance" (II Peter 3:9, NKJV). "Whoever desires [may] take the water of life freely" (Revelation 22:17, NKJV).

The requirement to receive the blessings of the new covenant is faith. If someone who has turned away from the Lord finds new faith, there is no biblical reason he could not enter anew into the blessings of the new covenant. James wrote, "Brethren, if anyone among you wanders from the truth, and someone turns him back, let him know that he who turns a sinner from the error of his way will save a soul from death and cover a multitude of sins" (James 5:19-20, NKJV).

Third, the issue for Esau at this point was not salvation but the birthright. The birthright gave the eldest son social precedence over any younger brothers (Genesis 43:33) and an inheritance twice that of any younger brother (Deuteronomy 21:27; Genesis 48:22; I Chronicles 5:1). By definition, this position was available to only one brother, but it had nothing to do with salvation. That is, the possibility of salvation was not limited to the first-born son who was in possession of the birthright.

When Hebrews says Esau "found no place for repentance," it may simply mean that there was no possibility Isaac could have second thoughts and take the birthright blessing from Jacob and restore it to Esau. The Greek *metanoias*, translated "repentance," means to "think afterwards" or to "change one's mind." Although Esau begged his father to bless him, the nature of the blessing rendered it impossible for Isaac to do so, although he did give Esau a less significant blessing. (See Genesis 27:39-40.) In other words, it was not Esau who could not repent—indeed, he definitely had a change of mind—it was Isaac.[89] If, on the other hand, Esau's inability to find a place for repentance refers not to Isaac but to himself, it means that he could find no way to reverse the consequences of his actions. The verse does not say that Esau could not repent; it is evident that he did. Rather, it says, in an unusual phrase, "he found no *place* for *repentance*" (Greek, *metanoias gar topon ouch euren*). What he sought diligently with tears was not the ability to repent, but a way, or a "place" (*topon*) to undo what he had done. But that was impossible.

Likewise, if a Christian commits apostasy, it is impossible to undo the commission of this sin. But it is pressing this reference to Esau too far to say some people cannot be saved regardless of how desperately they want to be. As Leon Morris pointed out in his commentary on this verse, "it is not a question of forgiveness. God's forgiveness is always open to the penitent. Esau could have come back to God. But he could not undo his act."[90] Westcott pointed out, "The son who had sacrificed his right could not undo the past, and it is this only which is in question. No energy of sorrow or self-condemnation, however sincere, could restore to him the prerogative of the first-born. The consideration of the forgiveness of his sin against God, as distinct from the reversal of the temporal consequences of his sin, lies wholly without [outside] the argument."[91]

The word "blessing" is translated from the Greek *eulogian*, which has to do with some kind of "good word." In this case, the blessing upon Jacob consisted of promises of material prosperity and social prominence (Genesis 27:28-29). In terms of the new covenant, the blessing is the gospel itself.

D.

A Contrast between the Old Covenant and the New (12:18-29)

(18) For ye are not come unto the mount that might be touched, and that burned with fire, nor unto blackness, and darkness, and tempest, (19) and the sound of a trumpet, and the voice of words; which voice they that heard intreated that the word should not be spoken to them any more: (20) (for they could not endure that which was commanded, And if so much as a beast touch the mountain, it shall be stoned, or thrust through with a dart: (21) and so terrible was the sight, that Moses said, I exceedingly fear and quake:) (22) but ye are come unto mount Sion, and unto the city of the living God, the heavenly Jerusalem, and to an innumerable company of angels, (23) to the general assembly and church of the firstborn, which are written in heaven, and to God the Judge of all, and to the spirits of just men made perfect, (24) and to Jesus the mediator of the new covenant, and to the blood of sprinkling, that speaketh better things than that of Abel. (25) See that ye refuse not him that speaketh. For if they escaped not who refused him that spake on earth, much more shall not we escape, if we turn away from him that speaketh from heaven: (26) whose voice then shook the earth: but now he hath

promised, saying, Yet once more I shake not the earth only, but also heaven. (27) And this word, Yet once more, signifieth the removing of those things that are shaken, as of things that are made, that those things which cannot be shaken may remain. (28) Wherefore we receiving a kingdom which cannot be moved, let us have grace, whereby we may serve God acceptably with reverence and godly fear: (29) for our God is a consuming fire.

Verses 18-21. Now begins a section, extending through verse 24, that compares the law of Moses to the new covenant. It clearly states the superiority of the new covenant.

The events to which these verses refer may be found in Exodus 19:12-13; 20:18-26 and Deuteronomy 4:11; 9:19. The mountain to which verse 18 refers is Mount Sinai, upon which God gave the law to Moses. The giving of the law was a dramatic event, characterized by tangible, visible, audible, earthly phenomena. These phenomena underscore that the law, which is not of faith (Galatians 3:12), had existed in an environment radically different from that of the new covenant. Faith does not demand visible evidence; it is convinced even of things that are still in the realm of hope (Hebrews 11:1). The new covenant also involves coming to a mountain, but one that human eyes have not yet seen (verse 22).

The description of the old covenant in these verses clearly casts it in a negative light. It was a physical mountain that burned and yet was shrouded in black darkness. (Compare the references to "outer darkness" in Matthew 8:12; 22:13; 25:30, 41. In at least the last reference, there is a parallel between "outer darkness" and "everlasting fire." It is possible for "fire" and "darkness" to exist in the same context.) God gave the law in the midst of a tempest. The trumpetlike voice they heard so frightened the people that they begged to hear it no more. They wanted Moses to relay the word of the Lord to them, rather than it coming to them directly. In other words, the law did not promote intimacy with God but distance from Him.

Although Mount Sinai could be touched, the people were forbidden to touch it. Indeed, if an animal or human being touched the mountain, the penalty was death by stoning or by being shot through with an arrow. (See Exodus 19:12-13.) The law was not given in an inviting and welcoming atmosphere. Everything about it struck fear in the hearts of the people and discouraged them from seeking intimacy with God. The sight was so terrifying that even Moses was "exceedingly afraid" and trembled.

Verses 22-24. The contrast between the two covenants is striking. Whereas God gave the law in a way that discouraged the people of Israel from hearing His voice and strictly forbade them even to touch the mountain upon which He gave the law, under the auspices of the new covenant believers are to "come boldly to the throne of grace" (Hebrews 4:16). They have "boldness to enter the Holiest by the blood of Jesus" (Hebrews 10:19).

Those who have placed their faith in Jesus Christ have come not to Mount Sinai but to Mount Zion. This is not the earthly Mount Zion that was captured by David from the Jebusites (II Samuel 5:6-9) and that was eventually extended to include the site of Solomon's Temple (Psalm 78:68-69),[92] but the heavenly Mount Zion, upon which stands the Lamb (Revelation 14:1). The earthly Mount

Zion was merely a type or shadow of the heavenly reality. (See 10:1.)

If Mount Zion refers specifically to the Temple which stood upon it, it is significant that the Temple of Solomon, in spite of its variations from the Tabernacle in the wilderness, was designed "by the Spirit" (I Chronicles 28:12). Concerning the plans for the Temple, David said, "All this . . . the LORD made me understand in writing, by His hand upon me" (I Chronicles 28:19, NKJV). If the Tabernacle was built according to a heavenly pattern (see 8:5; 9:23), there is no reason to think any less of the Temple.[93]

Believers have also come to "the city of the living God, the heavenly Jerusalem." John described this city in Revelation 21:2, 10-23. Paul also contrasted it with earthly Jerusalem. (See Galatians 4:25-26.) This is the city "which has foundations, whose builder and maker is God" (11:10). It is the city Abraham sought but never found. God has prepared it, however, for all people of faith (11:16). The heavenly Jerusalem is the continuing city that is to come (13:14). Although this city has not yet descended from heaven, those who partake of the new covenant have access to its spiritual privileges. (See 4:16; 9:8; 10:19-22.)

The heavenly Jerusalem is occupied by "an innumerable company of angels." This description reminds us that angels accompanied the giving of the law of Moses. (See 2:2.) Deuteronomy 33:2 speaks of "ten thousands of saints" that accompanied the Lord in the giving of the law, and the reference here is to angels. (See Septuagint translation.) The Hebrew *qadosh*, translated "saints" in Deuteronomy 33:2, certainly can refer to human beings, but there is nothing to prevent it from referring to angels.

The form of the word used in this verse simply means "holy ones." Since we know the law was given by the hands of angels, this is the most reasonable understanding of the word in Deuteronomy 33:2. According to Daniel, "ten thousand times ten thousand" stand before the Lord (Daniel 7:10), an obvious reference to the vast multitude of angels. At Sinai, the angels God used in giving the law were part of the distant and unapproachable scenario; in terms of the new covenant, it is not so. Believers have come to the heavenly city populated by the angels.

Believers have come also to "the general assembly and church of the firstborn." The words "assembly" (Greek, *panegyrei*) and "church" (Greek, *ekklesia*) in this context are virtual synonyms; by definition the church is an assembly of redeemed people. The word "firstborn" is plural (Greek, *prototokon*). (For the parallel between "firstborn" and "birthright," see comments on verse 16.) Under the new covenant, people of faith are the firstborn by virtue of their identification with Jesus Christ, who is the ultimate firstborn. (See 1:6; 2:13; Romans 8:29; Colossians 1:15, 18; Revelation 1:5.) Those who are in the church are "registered in heaven." Similar terminology appears elsewhere. Jesus told the seventy disciples that their names were written in heaven (Luke 10:20). Paul declared that the names of his fellow workers were in the Book of Life (Philippians 4:3). John said that those who were not written in the Book of Life would be cast into the lake of fire (Revelation 20:12, 15).

Believers have come to "God the Judge of all." At the giving of the law, the people of Israel were afraid even to hear the voice of God. Under the new covenant, people of faith have actually come to God Himself. The identification of God as "the Judge of all" no doubt reminded the first readers of this letter that they would one day answer to God for their response to the Messiah and His new covenant. (See 10:30-31.) If, after having received the knowledge of the truth, they trampled the Son of God underfoot (10:26, 29), they could expect to experience the vengeance of God. (See II Thessalonians 1:8.)

Believers have come to "the spirits of just men made perfect." This phrase apparently refers to the people of faith mentioned in chapter 11, who were justified by faith but who were not "made perfect apart from us" (11:40). Now that the new covenant has been established in Christ's blood, the full benefits of the Atonement have been applied to these people.

In general, when Scripture speaks of those who are dead without any reference to their material body, it identifies them as "spirits." When it refers to the dead with some awareness of their body, it tends describe them as "souls." (See, e.g., Revelation 6:9-10.) We should make no radical distinction between "soul" and "spirit." Both terms refer to the immaterial person, except in those cases where "soul" refers to the person himself in his full human existence. (See comments on 4:12.) It may be that "soul" emphasizes the immaterial person as he relates to his body and the material world, whereas "spirit" emphasizes the immaterial person as he relates to God. But the phrase "spirits of just men" does not establish a precise anthropology. It simply points out that those who died in faith now enjoy the perfection, or completeness, unavailable until the establishment of the new covenant.

Believers have come "to Jesus the mediator of the new

covenant." (On the concept of Jesus as the Mediator, see 8:6; 9:15.) The point is clear: no one can participate in the new covenant apart from faith in Jesus. The first readers of this letter were well acquainted with the concept of a new covenant from the Hebrew Scriptures. (See Jeremiah 31:31.) But they needed to know that if they turned away from Jesus, they were at the same time turning away from any hope of receiving the new covenant. (See 8:6.)

Believers have come to "the blood of sprinkling that speaks better things than that of Abel." The blood of sprinkling is the blood of Jesus, which established the new covenant. (See Matthew 26:28.) The blood of Jesus speaks of reconciliation to God, of forgiveness from sin. (See Ephesians 1:7.) The blood of Abel speaks of condemnation (Genesis 4:10). (For a discussion of "sprinkling," see comments on 10:22.)

The word "come" in verse 22 is the language of conversion. It is translated from the Greek *proseleluthate*, a form of which is transliterated "proselyte." Participants in the new covenant are those who have experienced the new birth (John 3:5). By means of this experience, they enjoy the privileges described in these verses.

We should not understand the references to "God the Judge" and "Jesus the mediator" as suggesting a distinction between "persons" in the Godhead. They do not mean one "person" in the Godhead is the Judge, while another is the Mediator. Jesus declared, "For the Father judges no one, but has committed all judgment to the Son . . . and has given Him authority to execute judgment also, because He is the Son of Man" (John 5:22, 27, NKJV). To the men of Athens, Paul said, "God . . . commands all men everywhere to repent, because He has appointed a day on which He will judge the world in righteousness by the Man whom he has ordained. He has given assurance of this to all by raising Him from the dead" (Acts 17:30-31, NKJV). On the basis of the Incarnation, by virtue of the genuineness and fullness of His humanity, which enables Him to identify with the human condition (4:15), God will judge all people.

References to God as Father pertain to God prior to, beyond, and above the Incarnation. Theologians use the term "transcendence" to speak of God in His "otherness" or "beyondness" or in contrast to His "immanence," which pertains to His presence among us. In relation to His immanence, God is identified as Spirit. But Jesus is God incarnate, God in human existence. We do not say, however, that God is at one point Father but not Son or Spirit, at another point Son but not Father or Spirit, and at another point Spirit but not Father or Son. All that God is, He is at all times. He does not change (Malachi 3:6). There has never been any change in God as it pertains to His essential nature or deity.

But we cannot deny that the Incarnation occurred at a specific point in time. The Incarnation did not effect any change in God as far as His divine essence was concerned, but it did result in God adding human existence to His divine nature. (See Philippians 2:5-8.) Before the Incarnation, God was eternally Father, Word, and Holy Spirit. (See John 1:1-2.) These titles do not designate three "persons" but describe one God who is at once Father of creation in a general sense and of people of faith in a specific sense, Word (Greek, *logos*) in reference to the communication of His purpose, and Spirit in reference to His activity. In the Incarnation, the Word was made flesh (John 1:14; I Timothy 3:16; I John 1:1-2; 4:1-2). This union of humanity and deity, Jesus Christ, became known as the Son of God. (See Luke 1:35; Galatians 4:4.) Thus, following the Incarnation, it is correct to speak of God as Father, Son, and Holy Spirit (Matthew 28:19). We can consider God as Father and as Holy Spirit apart from the Incarnation, for these are references to God in His transcendence and immanence. But when we consider the Son of God, we must always have the Incarnation in view, for He is by definition the Word made flesh.

Since the Incarnation, it is impossible to know the Father apart from knowing the Son. (See John 8:19.) To know Jesus is to know the Father; to see Jesus is to see the Father. (See John 14:6-10; I John 2:23.) There is no radical distinction of "persons" in God; the only distinction is between the humanity and deity of Christ. The "subject-object" relationship between the Father and the Son, which some trinitarian theologians use to prove a plurality of "persons" in the Godhead, actually arises from the fullness and genuineness of the humanity of the Messiah. We do not say one "nature" communicated with another, but the Incarnation required that Jesus possess a full human identity, including the human psyche. Because Jesus was fully human, He shared in all the experiences common to humans, including the need to pray. The Incarnation transcends our human experience and reasoning ability. We certainly cannot explain it by saying one "person" in the Godhead prayed to another.

Paul wrote, "For there is one God and one Mediator between God and men, the Man Christ Jesus" (I Timothy 2:5, NKJV). Any reference to Jesus as Mediator is an acknowledgement of His humanity. Any reference to God as Judge subsequent to the Incarnation is also a reference to God as He is known in the person of Jesus Christ. Thus, both verses 23 and 24 acknowledge the Incarnation, which is specifically the point that the first readers of Hebrews were in danger of denying. (See 10:29.)

Verse 25. Here again is an allusion to the danger facing the first readers of this book. Although they had placed their faith in Jesus and embraced the new covenant, they were in danger of reverting back to the rituals of the law of Moses. There seems to be a parallel here with 2:2-4, bracketing within this letter the impossibility of escaping the consequences of neglecting the new covenant. On Sinai, God spoke through angels (2:2; Galatians 3:19; Psalm 68:17). Under the new covenant, it is God Himself who speaks directly (verse 23 and 2:3). Those who heard and refused His voice (through angels) as expressed under the law of Moses did not escape the consequences of their disobedience (2:2); neither shall those who "turn away from Him" under the terms of the new covenant (2:3).

It is significant that the giving of the law involved God speaking (through angels) "on earth," while the new covenant involves God speaking "from heaven." This contrast indicates the nature of the covenants. The law of Moses was a covenant regulating the life of ancient Israel on earth, specifically in the land promised to Abraham. It contained no promise of eternal life in heaven. (See comments on 9:15.) The new covenant offers profuse promises of the eternal heavenly inheritance.[94] Even though the Hebrew Scriptures indicate that God did speak from heaven (Exodus 20:22; Deuteronomy 4:36), the writer of

Hebrews declares that it was "on earth" because God gave the covenant on a physical mountain on earth (verse 18) and it pertained to the earthly life of the people. It was "an earthly revelation in comparison with the revelation given in the gospel."[95]

The warning not to "turn away" is in harmony with all this letter has to say about the temptation facing its original readers. They had believed on Jesus as their Messiah, and they had come to Him on the basis of the new covenant, but they were now tempted to turn away and to revert back to the law of Moses.

There is a direct contextual and linguistic connection between the word translated "speaks" (Greek, *lalounta*) in this verse and "speaks" (Greek, *lalounti*) in verse 24. Both are from the Greek *laleo*, and their close connection here makes their meaning virtually synonymous. That is, what God speaks now in terms of the new covenant is the same as what the blood of Jesus speaks; it is a message of faith and forgiveness. There seems also to be a contextual parallel between the message spoken by the blood of Abel and that spoken by angels on God's behalf at Sinai, especially when we consider the extended context of verses 18-21. If we remember that the law of Moses was not of faith (Galatians 3:12) and that its emphasis was not so much on what one believed but on what one did, it seems clear that the result of the law was to condemn and to cry out for judgment, just as the blood of Abel did. (See Romans 7:5, 8-14.)

The Abrahamic covenant, which was separate from the law of Moses, addressed the need for faith. (See Galatians 3:6-19.) Nothing prevented the ancient Israelites from having faith in God; indeed, faith was the nature of the

Abrahamic covenant of which they were recipients. But the law of Moses itself had to do with works, not faith (Galatians 3:12). So the new covenant speaks of faith and forgiveness, while the law of Moses speaks of works and judgment. For those who turn away from the new covenant and defect to the old covenant, only the curse of the law—the demand for perfect obedience as the only means to avoid the negative consequences of the law—remains. (See Galatians 3:10-11.) There can be no escaping it.

Verses 26-28. At the giving of the law of Moses, the voice of God (through angels) shook the earth. (See Exodus 19:18.) Since the old covenant itself was an earthly covenant, the phenomena associated with it were essentially earthly. (See verses 18-21, 25.) But the new covenant is heavenly in nature, and God has promised that He will "once more . . . shake not only the earth, but also heaven." These words are drawn from Haggai 2:6, and as in Haggai, they indicate the termination of the law of Moses and the inauguration and permanence of the new covenant.

The "things that are being shaken" are the things pertaining to the law of Moses. They are being shaken in order to be removed. The law of Moses involves "things that are made." These things include the Tabernacle and all its furnishings; they even include the stone tablets made by Moses. (See Exodus 25:8-40; 26; 27; 28; 30; 31; 34:1; Hebrews 8:5-13.) Although the Temple still stood in Jerusalem when this letter was written, it would soon be destroyed by the invading Roman armies. Even as this letter was written, all remaining vestiges of the law of Moses were being shaken in preparation for their final removal.

But not only was the earth being shaken; so was heaven. This comment suggests that not only were the earthly expressions of the law of Moses being removed, the law was no longer bound in heaven. (See Matthew 16:19.)

The new covenant, however, could not be shaken. It is the final, ultimate covenant, made permanent by being established in the blood of Jesus (verse 24). It has been bound in heaven. This is the "kingdom which cannot be shaken." It does not have to do with "eating and drinking, but righteousness and peace and joy in the Holy Spirit" (Romans 14:17, NKJV). "Eating and drinking," as well as the declaration in Hebrews that our hearts should "be established by grace, not with foods which have not profited those who have been occupied with them" (13:9, NKJV), have to do with one of the distinctives of the law of Moses: the regulations on food and drink. The kingdom we are receiving is not characterized by earthly regulations (Colossians 2:20-23) but by grace that works through faith (Ephesians 2:7-9). On the basis of grace alone can we "serve God acceptably with reverence and godly fear."

Paul ministered according to the grace given to him by God. (See Galatians 2:7-9; Ephesians 3:7-8; Romans 12:3; 15:15; I Corinthians 15:10.) The word "grace" is translated from the Greek *charis*, which means a free gift of some kind. In other words, Paul's ministry flowed out of the exercise of the specific gift he received from God. In Paul's case, his gift was to be an apostle to the Gentiles.

But Paul was not unique in having a gift. To the church at Rome, he wrote, "Having then gifts differing according to the grace that is given to us, let us use them . . ."

(Romans 12:6, NKJV). In other words, God has given each believer a specific gift or gifts to define his or her function in the body of Christ. Along with this gift comes specific desires and abilities. (See Philippians 2:13; I Peter 4:10-11.)

On *eulabeias*, translated "godly fear," see comments on 5:7, where the identical word appears. The idea communicated by "reverence" (Greek, *deous*) is "awe." Under the new covenant, these are the only acceptable attitudes in our service to God, as opposed to the stark terror (Greek, *ekphobos*) and physical trembling that smote even Moses in conjunction with the law (verse 21).

The present participle translated "are receiving" (Greek, *paralambanontes*) implies that though we have begun to enjoy the provisions of the kingdom of God, we have not yet entered into its final and ultimate form. There is much more to come. (See I Corinthians 2:9-10.)

Verse 29. This verse is drawn from Deuteronomy 4:24. There the statement "For the LORD your God is a consuming fire, a jealous God" (NKJV) immediately follows a warning not to forget the covenant God established with Israel at Sinai: "Take heed to yourselves, lest you forget the covenant of the LORD your God which He made with you, and make for yourselves a carved image in the form of anything which the LORD your God has forbidden you" (Deuteronomy 4:23, NKJV). In its new context here in Hebrews, the essence of the warning is the same: Do not forget the covenant God has established with you. But in this new context, the reference to is the new covenant, not the law of Moses. Although Hebrews does not quote the entirety of Deuteronomy 4:24 here, saying that God is a consuming fire is equivalent to saying that He is a jealous God. We must not "turn away" from Jesus and the new covenant (verse 25), for God will not tolerate rivals. Those who refuse Him will not escape the consequences of their actions (verse 25; 2:3).

IV.

Practical Christianity
(13:1-25)

To this point, the letter to the Hebrews has been heavily weighted toward doctrinal concerns. The major emphasis has been the superiority of Jesus Christ over all others, including the Hebrew prophets, the angels, Moses, Aaron, Joshua, and the Levitical priesthood. Incorporated into this theme has been the superiority of the new covenant established by Jesus Christ over the law of Moses. This emphasis served the purpose of encouraging the first readers of the letter to remain true to Christ and not to defect to the old covenant.

That theme still undergirds chapter 13 (see verses 9-16, 20), but it occurs in the context of practical Christianity. What is the impact of the new covenant on daily Christian experience? It results in expressions of genuine love for one's brothers and sisters (verse 1), for strangers (verse 2), for imprisoned believers (verse 3), and for one's spouse (verse 4). It produces contentment and confidence in God (verse 5), respect for and submission to spiritual leaders (verses 7, 17, 24), doctrinal stability (verses 8-9), and a life characterized by thanksgiving and doing good (verses 15-16).

It may seem at first that verses 1-5 form a series of disconnected, unrelated maxims. But these introductory verses are actually tied together by the theme of love. Verse 1 exhorts the readers to "let brotherly love continue." "Brotherly love" is translated from the Greek *philadelphia*, a compound word formed from *philos* ("love") and *adelphos* ("brother.) In verse 2, the word translated "entertain" is the Greek *philoxenias*, formed from *philos* and *xenizo* ("to receive as a guest," "to entertain"). In verse 5, the words "without covetousness" are translated from the Greek *aphilargyros*, formed from *philos* and *argyros* ("silver"). So verse 1 has to do with loving one's brothers, verse 2 has to do with the demonstration of love in showing hospitality to strangers, and verse 5 declares there is to be no love of money in the lifestyle of the believer. Although verses 3 and 4 do not contain the word *philos* in any form, it is evident that love is their theme also, first in love for imprisoned believers and second in the honorable love for one's spouse that should characterize marriage.

A.

Love Others
(13:1)

(1) Let brotherly love continue.

Exhortations to brotherly love occur elsewhere in Romans 12:10, I Thessalonians 4:9, I Peter 1:22 and II Peter 1:7. The biblical idea of love is not limited to, or even chiefly characterized by, one's feelings or emotional attachments. Rather, we cannot separate love from behavior. In its active sense, *philos*, from which *philadelphia* ("brotherly love") comes, means to be "loving, kindly disposed, devoted."[96] Contextually, brotherly love includes hospitality to strangers (verse 2), identification with imprisoned believers (verse 3), and faithfulness to one's marriage vows (verse 4).

Ellingworth pointed out that "Hebrews does not distinguish sharply between [*philadelphia*] and [*agape*]: [*agape*], too, is a human activity directed towards fellow-Christians."[97] References to *agape* ("love") appear in 6:10 and 10:24.

The concept of the brotherhood of believers also appears in 3:1 and 13:23. But in Hebrews, believers are not brothers with one another only; they are also Christ's brethren (2:11, 12, 17).

The admonition to "let brotherly love continue" may be

a response to the possible defection of first-century Jewish believers from Christ to the law of Moses. If they turned away from Christ, they would be turning away from the brotherhood they found in Him. They should focus on their new identity as brethren in Christ rather than on their previous identity as members of the Jewish community. They should allow the love that characterized the new believing community at the first to continue.

B.

Entertain Strangers
(13:2)

(2) Be not forgetful to entertain strangers: for thereby some have entertained angels unawares.

The word translated "entertain" (Greek, *philoxenias*) means to show hospitality. Among the ancient Hebrews, hospitality was a great virtue. (See Isaiah 58:7.) A good example was Abraham, who showed hospitality to three "men," two of whom turned out to be angels and one of whom was the Lord (Genesis 18:1-22). The statement "some have entertained angels unawares" no doubt refers to his experience. When he first received these visitors, he did not know they were celestial beings. Because of Abraham's willingness to show hospitality to these visitors, God blessed him with the promise of a son by Sarah.

Hospitality is equally important in the New Testament, which presents it as an expression of authentic Christianity. (See Romans 12:13; I Peter 4:9.) It is a requirement for spiritual leaders. (See I Timothy 3:2; Titus 1:8.) Jesus held up hospitality as evidence of love for one's neighbor (Luke 10:34).

It seems likely that the "strangers" were fellow believers in Christ who were traveling and in need of safe lodgings.[98] In the first century, public inns were of questionable reputation.[99] Even though they may not be personally acquainted with such travelers, believers should always stand ready to extend loving care to their brothers in Christ.

The admonition to "be not forgetful" may imply that as the early Jewish Christians began to lose their focus on their identity with Christ and to contemplate returning to their former life in Judaism, they became unconcerned with the needs of other Christians. The more focused they were on their identity with Christ, the more concerned they would be with the needs of those whose faith was common with theirs.

C.

Empathize with Those in Prison
(13:3)

(3) Remember them that are in bonds, as bound with them; and them which suffer adversity, as being yourselves also in the body.

A further expression of brotherly love is to look for opportunities to minister to imprisoned believers. (See Matthew 25:34-46.) It was not uncommon in the first century for Jewish Christians to be imprisoned for their faith. (See Romans 16:7; Colossians 4:10; Philemon 23.) Paul had this experience and deeply appreciated the support of believers (Philippians 1:7, 13; 4:10-14).

The phrase "and them which suffer adversity" does not mean two groups are in view here, one in prison and the other suffering adversity. The word "and" is not in the Greek text; the translators supplied it. The phrase "them which suffer adversity" further describes "them that are in bonds." The imprisoned believers were enduring hardship.

In the earlier days of their faith, the first recipients of this letter had shown compassion on the author of the letter in his imprisonment (10:32-34). It may be that they had lapsed in this concern due to their flagging faith. They should "call to remembrance the former days"

(10:32) and remember those in prison as they had previously done.

Proper empathy would arise as they identified so completely with their imprisoned brethren as to consider themselves "bound with them." The nature of the Christian community is that when "one member suffers, all the members suffer with it" (I Corinthians 12:26, NKJV).

We may be tempted to find in the phrase "as being yourselves also in the body" a reference to the church as the body of Christ. But that would be to read something into the text.[100] Rather, the point is that since every human being exists in a human body, it is possible to envision how we would feel if we experienced the same adversity as our imprisoned brethren.

D.

Avoid Moral Impurity
(13:4)

(4) Marriage is honourable in all, and the bed undefiled: but whoremongers and adulterers God will judge.

One of the false doctrines which attacked first century Christians was that celibacy is superior to marriage. (See I Timothy 4:1-3.) This notion ignores that marriage is God's idea; He said it is not good for man to be alone. (See Genesis 2:18, 21-24.) Solomon declared that a man who finds "a wife findeth a good thing, and obtaineth favour of the Lord" (Proverbs 18:22). Jesus demonstrated the honorableness of marriage by participating in a wedding celebration, where He worked His first miracle (John 2:1-11).

Within the covenant bonds of marriage, the sexual relationship is wholesome. To become "one flesh" is as pertinent to marriage as to leave one's father and mother and to enter into the vows of permanence. (See Genesis 2:24.) Indeed, husband and wife are not to refrain from the sexual relationship unless both consent, and then only for a brief period of time (I Corinthians 7:3-5).

In contrast to the sexual relationship in marriage, any sexual activity outside of marriage is certain to merit the judgment of God. "Whoremongers" is translated from the Greek *pornous* and refers specifically to fornication. It is a broad word that encompasses sexual immorality of all kinds, while the word "adultery" refers specifically to the unfaithfulness of those who are married to their vows wherein they promised to keep themselves exclusively to their spouse.[101] Thus, adultery is a form of fornication, but fornication includes more than adultery. Neither fornicators nor adulterers shall inherit the kingdom of God (I Corinthians 6:9; Ephesians 5:2-6; Galatians 5:19-21).

It is possible to translate this verse as "Let marriage be honorable . . . and let the bed be undefiled." This option is due to the emphatic position of *timios*, translated "honourable." In this case, the point would be that all believers are to highly prize marriage, and they are to refuse to defile the legitimate sexual relationship by being unfaithful to their vows and failing to keep themselves exclusively for one another.[102] (See Matthew 19:9.)

E.

Avoid Greed
(13:5-6)

(5) Let your conversation be without covetousness; and be content with such things as ye have: for he hath said, I will never leave thee, nor forsake thee. (6) So that we may boldly say, The Lord is my helper, and I will not fear what man shall do unto me.

The Greek word translated "conversation" in the KJV is *tropos*, which means "conduct" or "way of life." "Without covetousness" is translated from the Greek *aphilargyros*, which is formed from *philos* ("love") and *argyros* ("silver"). The Christian life is to be characterized by love for one's brethren (verse 1), strangers (verse 2), prisoners (verse 3), and one's spouse (verse 4), but it is not to be characterized by a love for money. Instead, in reference to material things, believers are to be content with their present circumstances. (See Philippians 4:11.) Contentment should certainly characterize the lives of those who have food and clothing (I Timothy 6:6-8). These are the essential necessities of life; anything beyond food and clothing is a luxury.

This admonition may be connected to the temptation the original readers faced to return to the law of Moses. The law promised wealth to those who obeyed its requirements.

(See Deuteronomy 8:18; 28:4-6, 8, 11-13.) These Jewish Christians may have looked with longing back to the covenant that promised plenty of material goods. Instead, they should have recognized that knowing God is sufficient. As Jesus taught, life is not defined by material possessions (Luke 12:15). The same word translated "without covetousness" here appears in I Timothy 3:3, which declares that a bishop must not be greedy for money. Indeed, the desire for riches brings many unnecessary and destructive temptations (I Timothy 6:9). Scripture does not oppose hard work, saving, and planning for the future, but it does oppose greed and miserliness. The love of money can actually cause a person to stray from the faith (I Timothy 6:10). It may be that this was at least part of the danger facing the original readers of Hebrews.

The statement "I will never leave you nor forsake you" comes from Deuteronomy 31:8 and Joshua 1:5. In both contexts, God gave the promise in view of the challenge before Joshua to take the land promised to the fathers. As he looked to new horizons and achievements, Joshua had the promise that the Lord would not forsake Him. It is significant that the same promise is given here to Jewish Christians at an equally critical juncture in their experience: Would they press on into the fullness of new covenant faith and experience, or would they fearfully turn back to what they had known and to what was comfortable to them? (See 6:1-2.) God was with Joshua and the people of Israel as they crossed the River Jordan into the fulfillment of the promises made to the patriarchs, and He would be with these Jewish Christians as they pressed on in pursuit of the blessings of the new covenant promised through the Hebrew prophets.

In verse 6, the Septuagint translation of Psalm 118:6 appears. This quote may come in response to pressures brought against the first readers of this letter by unbelieving relatives and former companions in the "Jews' religion" (Galatians 1:13). (See 10:32-33; 12:3-4; Matthew 10:34-36.) It may be that the early Jewish Christians were intimidated by the enmity of unbelieving Jews to the point that their resolve was weakening. If this was the case, they should boldly proclaim the promise of Psalm 118:6: "The LORD is my helper, and I will not fear what man shall do unto me." When people of faith are walking in obedience to the Word of God, they have assurance of the help of the Lord. They do not have a guarantee of freedom from pain or difficulty, but God promises to help them through all trials. When God is our help, nothing anyone can do will ultimately contribute to our downfall. (See Romans 8:18, 28-39.)

F.

Follow Your Leaders
(13:7-8)

(7) Remember them which have the rule over you, who have spoken unto you the word of God: whose faith follow, considering the end of their conversation. (8) Jesus Christ the same yesterday, and to day, and for ever.

Three times this chapter refers to those who "rule." (See also verses 17 and 24.) The word translated "rule" (Greek, *hegoumenon*) has to do with leading or guiding. The idea is not so much that of commanding but of leading by example. (See I Peter 5:1-3.) We see this idea in that those who rule are those who have "spoken . . . the word of God." They are people whose faith should be followed as believers consider the end result of their conduct. These people have not merely told others what they should do; they have patterned the lifestyle that should be common to all believers.

The ministry of these people undoubtedly falls into the categories of Ephesians 4:11. They have spoken the Word of God, which is the responsibility of bishops (I Timothy 3:2). Bishops are also known as elders (Titus 1:5, 7). The ministry of bishops or elders fulfills at least the roles of pastors and teachers.

Apparently, the temptation to defect from Christ and His new covenant had not affected the spiritual leaders of the people to whom this letter was first written. There is no indication that their faith was in danger. Indeed, their faith was an example to follow. In the face of their temptations, the first readers of this letter were to keep in mind or think of (Greek, *mnemoneuete*, from we derive the English "mnemonics") their spiritual leaders. The leaders were not turning away from Christ. The believers needed to examine carefully the end result of the life of faith of which their leaders were exemplars. Those who maintained their faith would enjoy all the rich, eternal blessings of the new covenant; these were too precious to trade for the temporal attraction of Judaism.

In order to grasp the significance of verse 8 within its context, it is necessary to look at the verse and its surroundings from the viewpoint of first-century Jewish Christians. The statement "Jesus Christ, the same yesterday, and to day, and for ever" would no doubt have reminded them of Malachi 3:6: "For I am the LORD, I do not change; therefore you are not consumed, O sons of Jacob" (NKJV). Malachi gave the immutability of the Lord as the only reason He had not already consumed the disobedient, unbelieving Israelites. The failure of Israel to obey the law of Moses had placed them in danger of the judgment of God (Malachi 3:5), but His unchanging mercy had prevailed over judgment. God continued to spare them to give them an opportunity to repent and to keep the commandments.

Hebrews 13 addresses the practical aspects of obedience to the new covenant. In the immediate context of verse 8, there is an admonition for believers to live as their spiritual leaders (verse 7) and to resist strange doctrines (verse 8). Like the Israelites in the days of Malachi, the first readers of this letter were tempted to abandon God's covenant. For Malachi's readers, the covenant in view was the law of Moses. For the readers of Hebrews, the covenant in view was the new covenant. But in both cases, the only reason the judgment of God had not already fallen on the disobedient was His immutability. People may change; they may become unfaithful. But God does not change; His mercy endures. (See Psalm 136.)

The immutability of Jesus Christ (or the fact that He does not change) is strong evidence of His deity. Only God does not change. That the author declared "Jesus Christ" is the same yesterday, today, and forever rather than simply asserting the Lord does not change indicates anew that believers must not trample the Son of God underfoot (10:29). To embrace the new covenant was not an option; the identity of Jesus Christ made it necessary to remain faithful to Him and the new covenant.

G.

Avoid Judaism; Follow Jesus
(13:9-14)

(9) Be not carried about with divers and strange doctrines. For it is a good thing that the heart be established with grace; not with meats, which have not profited them that have been occupied therein. (10) We have an altar, whereof they have no right to eat which serve the tabernacle. (11) For the bodies of those beasts, whose blood is brought into the sanctuary by the high priest for sin, are burned without the camp. (12) Wherefore Jesus also, that he might sanctify the people with his own blood, suffered without the gate. (13) Let us go forth therefore unto him without the camp, bearing his reproach. (14) For here have we no continuing city, but we seek one to come.

Here, in the essence of simplicity, is a summary of the warning treated in great detail elsewhere in Hebrews: Believers in Christ are not to be moved by divers ("various") and strange doctrines. (See Ephesians 4:14.) Specifically, they are not to revert to any aspect of Judaism. "Meats" refers to the commandments in the law of Moses pertaining to diet. Even these were mere shadows fulfilled in Christ. (See Colossians 2:16-17.) Commandments having to do with foods are contrasted here with grace. The law of Moses focused on human behavior, not on the grace of God. (See John 1:17; Galatians 3:12; Romans 3:21-24; 11:6.)

One of the "strange doctrines" that attacked the first-century church was the commandment to abstain from certain foods, which God "created to be received with thanksgiving by those who believe and know the truth" (I Timothy 4:3, NKJV). Contrary to the restrictions in the law of Moses, the foods God created to be received with thanksgiving include "every creature of God" (I Timothy 4:4). Prior to the law of Moses, God said to Noah, "Every moving thing that lives shall be food for you" (Genesis 9:3, NKJV).

God gave ancient Israel the laws limiting their diet not primarily for health reasons but to provide another point of separation between them and the heathen nations about them. (See Leviticus 11:44-47.) The Canaanites considered the pig the holiest creature, the choice sacrifice to offer to their idols. As part of the separation between Israel and the Canaanites, God commanded the Israelites to consider the pig to be unclean. But with the end of the law of Moses, the restrictions on diet were lifted, and the situation returned to its pre-Mosaic state in which every moving thing was as acceptable for food as vegetables were. Jesus declared this concept when He said, "Do you not perceive that whatever enters a man from outside cannot defile him, because it does not enter his heart but his stomach, and is eliminated, thus purifying all foods?" (Mark 7:18-19, NKJV). In a vision, God told Peter to eat all manner of animals. Although the purpose was to tell him to preach to the Gentiles, certainly a holy God would not have used something inherently unholy to represent something He had cleansed. (See Acts 10:10-15.)

The focus of the new covenant is on the heart, not the physical body. The only way one's heart can be established is by grace. To be occupied with regulations concerning food is of no profit. Food "does not commend us to God; for neither if we eat are we the better, nor if we do not eat are we the worse" (I Corinthians 8:8, NKJV). "The kingdom of God is not eating and drinking, but righteousness and peace and joy in the Holy Spirit" (Romans 14:17, NKJV). In other words, the concerns of the kingdom of God do not involve one's diet. The heart has to do with the inner person; food has to do with the outer person. The new covenant centers on the grace of God (Ephesians 2:8-9). As believers focus on God's grace, they will be firmly established in their spiritual life. But a focus on the outer person contributes nothing to the spiritual life. (See 9:10.)

Participants in the new covenant have access to an altar that is off-limits to those who are still occupied with the rituals of the law of Moses. As in other cases throughout Hebrews, verse 10 points out the impossibility of merging the new covenant and the old covenant. Those who continue to "serve the tabernacle," which represents all aspects of the law of Moses, have no right to the blessings of the new covenant. To participate in the new covenant, one must recognize the fulfillment and termination of the law of Moses in Christ Jesus (Romans 10:4).

The word "altar" here does not refer to a literal, physical altar; it is a figure of speech that represents the sacrifice of Jesus Christ.[103] The cross of Christ demands exclusive allegiance. It cannot be added to the law, for it brings the law to an end and replaces it with an entirely new covenant. (See Colossians 2:14; Ephesians 2:14-15.)

On the Day of Atonement, the priests did not eat the bodies of the sacrificial animals as they did on other days (Leviticus 10:16-18); they carried them outside the camp of Israel and burned them (Leviticus 16:27). The sacrifices on the Day of Atonement represented the death of Jesus on the cross; the priests were not permitted to eat the flesh of these sacrifices. There was apparently a divinely ordained shadow here. Since the sacrifices of the Day of Atonement represented the death of Jesus, which would establish the new covenant, and since the new covenant requires separation from the rituals of the law of Moses, God ordained that the sacrifices of the Day of Atonement would be treated differently than the other sacrifices. If the priests had been permitted to eat the flesh of the bull and the goat offered on the Day of Atonement, it would suggest that the benefits of the new covenant come by the works of the law. But taking the bodies of these animals outside the camp and burning them implies the severance of the benefits of the new covenant from the rituals of the Tabernacle.

In fulfillment of this type, Jesus suffered outside the gate, or outside of the city of Jerusalem. Jerusalem represented in the broadest sense the law of Moses (Galatians 4:25). If Jesus had died inside the city, it could perhaps be said that He in some way perpetuated the law of Moses by simply being the ultimate sacrifice among many. But His sacrifice was in a category alone. It was not merely the greatest sacrifice; it was the only sacrifice ever offered that could actually remove sin. In order to "sanctify the people with his own blood," Jesus was crucified outside of the city that personified the law of Moses. (See comments on 10:10.) Therefore, those who wish to identify with Him and to partake of the benefits of the new covenant must turn from the law of Moses, depart from the earthly Jerusalem, and "go forth . . . unto him without the camp." To go outside the "camp" implies leaving the law behind. It is something done outside or external to the old covenant under which Israel lived. It is impossible to stay within the camp—to continue to identify with the law—and to go forth to Jesus at the same time.

A reproach is associated with turning away from the law and embracing Jesus as the Messiah. This reproach was particularly painful for the Jewish people. For Jesus to be taken outside of the city of Jerusalem to be crucified indicated that He was rejected by all that the city represented, which included centuries of tradition that exalted the law of Moses as the supreme revelation of God. The reproach is seen in the cry "Crucify Him!" It is seen in that He died the death reserved for the most base and despicable criminals. To the Jewish people who rejected Him, their peers who believed on Jesus were tainted with the same reproach.

For the Jewish believers who had turned their backs on the religious system represented by the city of Jerusalem, it should have been great comfort to know that Jerusalem was not the eternal city anyway. The "continuing city" is the one to come: the New Jerusalem. (See 11:10, 16.) Those who depart from earthly Jerusalem— and by implication from the law of Moses—to identify with Jesus Christ in His reproach have assurance of their inheritance in the heavenly city to come.

H.

Sacrifices of Praise and Doing Good (13:15-16)

(15) By him therefore let us offer the sacrifice of praise to God continually, that is, the fruit of our lips giving thanks to his name. (16) But to do good and to communicate forget not: for with such sacrifices God is well pleased.

The discussion of sacrifices in these verses served to draw the attention of the early Jewish Christians away from the sacrificial system of the old covenant and point them to the completely different sacrifices of the new covenant. Animal sacrifices were an essential feature of the law of Moses, and they were a consequence of sin. No animal sacrifice actually took away sins (10:4). Instead, they constantly reminded the Israelites of their sinfulness (10:3).

Under the new covenant, the only sacrifice related to sin is the death of Jesus on the cross (verse 12; see also 10:10, 14, 18). Participants in the new covenant do offer sacrifices, but not animal sacrifices to remind them of their sinfulness. Instead, they offer sacrifices of praise, doing good, and sharing. (The Greek *koinonias*, translated "communicate" by the KJV, means to have fellowship or to share with one another.)

We are to offer the sacrifice of praise—which we perform as we verbalize our thanksgiving to God— "continually." That is, praise is to characterize the life of the believer. We are to offer praise to God "by him," which contextually means by Jesus Christ. This statement is similar to Peter's admonition to "offer up spiritual sacrifices, acceptable to God by Jesus Christ" (I Peter 2:5). Peter is in harmony with the author of Hebrews here; the sacrifices we are to offer are radically different from those of the old covenant. They do not involve animals; they are spiritual in nature; we offer them to God as we focus our adoration exclusively on Jesus Christ. (See comments on 7:25.)

The phrase "the fruit of our lips giving thanks to his name" follows the Septuagint translation of Hosea 14:2. The KJV translates the Hebrew text of this passage as "so will we render the calves of our lips," with "calves" representing the offering of bullocks. Hosea saw this sacrifice of praise as happening in conjunction with the establishment of the new covenant with Israel. When the people return to God (Hosea 14:1) and their iniquity is taken away (this is new covenant language; see comments on Hebrews 10:16-17), their sacrifice of praise will involve vocalized praise rather than the blood of animals. By using this quotation, Hebrews asserts that those who have faith in Jesus Christ enjoy the blessing Hosea foretold. To turn away from Him would be to reject the promise Hosea gave.

Under the law of Moses, the sacrifice of thanksgiving involved the offering of an animal. (See Leviticus 7:11-38.) Not so under the new covenant. Even the Psalms anticipated a thanksgiving offering that did not involve the flesh of animals. (See Psalm 50:12-15.)

In verse 15 we see the Hebrew identification of God with His name. To give thanks to His name is to offer the sacrifice of praise to God Himself. To the Jewish mind, it was impossible to separate a person from his name. (See 1:4; 2:12; 6:10.) In a very real sense, a person was his name, and his name was the person.

Believers are to take advantage of every opportunity to do good, especially to fellow believers (Galatians 6:10). This admonition does not mean they are to have less concern about doing good for those outside the family of God, but they are never to miss an opportunity to do good for those who are in the household of faith. The fellowship that characterizes the believing life should include sharing with those in need. There is no room in the family of God for selfishness, greed, or hoarding. If a person sees his brother in need and has the resources to help but does nothing, the love of God is absent in his life (I John 3:17).

God is well pleased with the sacrifices these verses describe; He is not pleased with animal sacrifices offered by those who would revive or perpetuate the obsolete Mosaic covenant. (See 8:13; 10:6.)

The sacrifices just named are not the only ones associated with the new covenant. Other important sacrifices today are the believer's life (Romans 12:1; Philippians 2:17) and the results of evangelistic efforts, new converts (Romans 15:16).

I.

Obey Your Leaders
(13:17)

(17) Obey them that have the rule over you, and submit yourselves: for they watch for your souls, as they that must give account, that they may do it with joy, and not with grief: for that is unprofitable for you.

This is one of three references in chapter 13 to those who rule. (See verses 7 and 24.) As the comments on verse 7 point out, ruling does not mean dictatorship or domination, but leading by one's example of faith and by the declaration of the Word of God. Deviation from the declaration of God's Word disqualifies one from being a spiritual leader. Leaders are to be obeyed as they speak the Word of God and as they are exemplars of a life of faith.

But there can be no escaping that believers must obey their spiritual leaders who are faithful to the Word of God. They must "submit themselves" to their spiritual leaders.

The reason is clear: spiritual leaders are responsible to God for the souls of those they lead. They will give an account to God for their work. If those for whom they were responsible were obedient to the Word of God, these leaders can give an account to God with joy. If not, their report to Him will be with grief.

There is no indication here that the spiritual leader's eternal reward hinges on the faithfulness of those who follow him. The report of grief will not be unprofitable for the spiritual leader; it will be unprofitable for those who refused to obey.

This call to obey spiritual leaders is a call to be faithful to the new covenant. The leaders were not tempted to turn away from Christ and the new covenant; thus the believers should follow their example.

J.

Pray
(13:18-19)

(18) Pray for us: for we trust we have a good conscience, in all things willing to live honestly. (19) But I beseech you the rather to do this, that I may be restored to you the sooner.

The writer of Hebrews desired the prayers of those to whom he wrote; he especially wished them to pray that he could be restored to them quickly. This comment gives no definite information as to the identity of the author. We know nothing for certain as to why the writer was separated from his readers. It does not seem to be imprisonment, for he declared in verse 23 that Timothy has been set free from apparent imprisonment and that he would accompany Timothy if he came to see the original readers soon. If the writer were imprisoned, he would have had no assurance that he would be able to do so.

The human author of Hebrews was confident that he had a good conscience; he desired to live a completely honorable life. The Greek *peithometha*, translated "trust" by the KJV, means the writer was persuaded that this was so. The Greek word translated "honestly" by the KJV (*kalos*) means "good" in the sense of "honorable." The "good conscience" to which he testified contrasts with the "evil conscience" from which those who are cleansed by Christ's blood are delivered. (See 10:22.) In the larger context of Hebrews, the honorable life is the life of faith in Jesus Christ and adherence to the new covenant.

V.

Concluding Benedictions
(13:20-25)

(20) Now the God of peace, that brought again from the dead our Lord Jesus, that great shepherd of the sheep, through the blood of the everlasting covenant, (21) make you perfect in every good work to do his will, working in you that which is wellpleasing in his sight, through Jesus Christ; to whom be glory for ever and ever. Amen. (22) And I beseech you, brethren, suffer the word of exhortation: for I have written a letter unto you in few words. (23) Know ye that our brother Timothy is set at liberty; with whom, if he come shortly, I will see you. (24) Salute all them that have the rule over you, and all the saints. They of Italy salute you. (25) Grace be with you all. Amen.

The final verses of Hebrews are a fitting conclusion to a letter whose chief purpose is to demonstrate the superiority of Jesus Christ over all previous revelations of God and to encourage its readers to remain true to the new covenant rather than defecting to Mosaism. This section acknowledges the resurrection of Jesus from the dead, a historical fact that demands a response and that is the evidence of the inauguration of the new covenant (verse 20). It identifies Jesus as the great Shepherd of the sheep, a description that no doubt reminded the early Jewish readers of the new covenant promises associated with the regathering of the nation (verse 20). The covenant established on the basis of Jesus' blood is the everlasting, or eternal, covenant, in obvious contrast to the temporary covenant God made with Israel at Sinai (verse 20).

The closing verses also indicate that the works associated with the new covenant are actually performed in the believer by the God of peace (verse 21). The law was weak through the flesh (Romans 8:3); it made demands upon the ancient Israelites but offered no enablements. Not so with the new covenant.

So from beginning to end, the Book of Hebrews is faithful to its central theme: Jesus Christ is better than all else, and the new covenant established in His blood is vastly superior to the law of Moses.

Verses 20-21. The concluding benediction expresses the writer's hope that God will bring his readers to completion by performing in them the things that please Him. It acknowledges that this work will take place "through Jesus Christ," who deserves eternal glory.

The sentiment of these verses is in keeping with all that we discover about the new covenant elsewhere in Scripture.

The resurrection of Jesus from the dead signaled the inauguration of the new covenant. (See Acts 2:22-33; 13:29-41; Romans 1:1-6; Isaiah 53:8-11—even though He is "cut off from the land of the living," the Messiah's days are "prolonged" so He can "see His seed"; Matthew 12:38-40; 16:1-4; Luke 11:29-32; I Corinthians 15:3-4, 14, 17-19.) It is impossible to remain passive in the face of Christ's resurrection. If we do not accept the biblical claim that Jesus rose from the dead and acknowledge the legitimacy of the new covenant He inaugurated, the only alternative is to trample the Son of God underfoot, count the blood of the covenant a common thing, and insult the Spirit of grace. (See 10:29.)

The description of Jesus as "that great Shepherd of the sheep" is new covenant language. As opposed to Moses, who served as a shepherd to Israel from the Exodus to his death (Isaiah 63:11), and Cyrus, a Gentile king who temporarily served as Israel's shepherd in a limited way (Isaiah 44:28), Jesus Christ is the "great," and thus the ultimate and final, Shepherd. This role fulfills the prophecy of Ezekiel concerning the regathering of the people of Israel into their land with one shepherd over them. (See Ezekiel 34:11-31, especially verses 13 and 23.) Jesus claimed to be the Good Shepherd who gives His life for the sheep (John 10:11-18.) Even in this context, the resurrection of Jesus from the dead is central (John 10:18). Jesus, whose resurrection gives us a "living hope," is the Chief Shepherd (I Peter 1:3, 7; 5:4.)

The phrase "the blood of the everlasting covenant" is unmistakably a reference to the new covenant. The blood of Jesus stands in contrast to the blood of bulls and goats that characterized the covenant God established with Israel at Sinai and that was temporary in nature (8:9, 13; 10:4, 16-17, 19; Exodus 24:8; Jeremiah 31:32). The prophecies of the Hebrew Scriptures identify the new covenant as an everlasting covenant (Isaiah 55:3; Jeremiah 32:40; Ezekiel 37:26). Although the Hebrew Scriptures also speak of an "everlasting covenant" when the new covenant is not in view, this use does not indicate that any other covenant will endure eternally.[104] The

Hebrew *olam*, translated "everlasting," can—given the right context—mean "eternal," but it does not necessarily have reference to something without end. *Olam* inherently means "a very long time." For example, the Aaronic priesthood was an "everlasting priesthood" (Exodus 40:15), but we discover in Hebrews 7:11-12 that it was not eternal; the termination of the law of Moses necessitated the termination of the Aaronic priesthood. The rituals associated with the Day of Atonement in ancient Israel were an "everlasting statute" (Leviticus 16:34), but they terminated with the death of Jesus Christ (Hebrews 10:4-18).

Regarding the "everlasting" covenants in the Hebrew Scriptures, only the context of these references and any related texts in the New Testament can tell us the significance of the word "everlasting." The New Testament itself, however, identifies only one covenant as "everlasting," and that is the new covenant. The Greek *aioniou*, translated "everlasting" in the KJV, means "eternal." The same word describes the eternal life that will be the reward of the righteous (Matthew 25:46). Specifically, the Book of Hebrews itself defines the covenant in view here: it is the same covenant addressed in 8:6. The writer of Hebrews declared that the old covenant was *not* eternal (7:11-12; 8:7-13; 9:10, 15; 10:9, 16-18). Therefore, the everlasting covenant must be the covenant that replaced it. The new covenant will never be superseded.

The phrase "make you perfect in every good work to do his will, working in you that which is wellpleasing in his sight" is in harmony with everything the New Testament says elsewhere about the grace of God under the new covenant working in believers to give them right desires and abilities. (See Philippians 2:13; I Corinthians 15:10; Galatians 2:7-9; Ephesians 3:7-8; Romans 12:3, 6; 15:15; I Peter 4:10-11.) By contrast, the law of Moses, which demanded perfect obedience (Galatians 3:10-12), was weak through the flesh (Romans 8:3). In other words, the law demanded of people what they could not do. Indeed, one of the purposes of the law was to convince the people of Israel that they were sinners in need of a Savior (Galatians 3:19-25; Romans 4:15; 5:20; 7:5-14; I Corinthians 15:56). On the other hand, the commandments of the new covenant are its enablements (Philippians 1:6; 2:13).

The word "perfect" is translated from *katartisai*, which means being "equipped." The same word appears in 10:5, where it is translated "prepared." The idea is that God will fully equip believers to do the things that please Him. In the new covenant are all the resources one needs to live a life pleasing to God.

All new covenant blessings come "through Jesus Christ." If He is rejected, there is no hope for salvation (10:26-31).

The phrase "forever and ever" is translated from *aionas ton aionon. Aionas* and *aionon* are from the same word translated "everlasting" in the phrase "the everlasting covenant." The covenant established in Christ's blood will endure for as long as He receives glory, and that is for eternity.

"Amen" is the English transliteration of the Greek transliteration of the Hebrew word, which means something like, "So be it!"

The identification of God as the "God of peace" reassured the troubled Hebrew Christians that in spite of their trials (12:3-4), they could find peace in God, but only under the terms of the new covenant, which the "God of peace" introduced by the resurrection of our Lord Jesus.

"The God of peace" is the One who "brought again from the dead our Lord Jesus." Elsewhere, Scripture declares that Jesus was raised from the dead by the Holy Spirit, the Spirit of God. (See Romans 1:4; 8:9, 11.) Because Jesus Christ is God, the Holy Spirit is also the Spirit of Christ. Thus there was no contradiction for Jesus to declare He would raise Himself. (See John 2:19-21.) When Scripture asserts that Jesus was raised from the dead by God, or by the Spirit of God, the emphasis is on Jesus as Messiah, a focus on the genuineness and fullness of His human nature. When Jesus declares He will raise Himself from the dead, the emphasis is on His deity.

Though God raised others from the dead and restored them to natural life, Jesus was raised to die no more (Romans 6:9-10). He was the prototype of all whom God would eventually raise from the dead to eternal life (I Corinthians 15:20). His resurrection from the dead was conclusive proof that He was who He claimed to be. (See Matthew 12:39-40.)

Verse 22. The letter to the Hebrews is a "word of exhortation." Exhortation has to do with encouragement. The purpose of the letter was to encourage the wavering Hebrew Christians not to lose heart. Though their trials were painful (12:3), it would have been a terrible mistake for them to turn away from Jesus Christ to return to the rituals of the law.

In this verse we see the wistful appeal of the author. Having written as clearly and persuasively as possible, now all he could do was appeal to his brethren—those who shared his faith in Christ—to receive his message.

Perhaps the reference to having written in "few words" implies that he could have written much more that would have been pertinent. On the other hand, *bracheon*, translated "few words," may suggest that the author was "outspoken," or bold.

Verse 23. Timothy had been imprisoned but was now released. The author's declaration that if Timothy came shortly to see the recipients of this letter he would come with Timothy, supports his appeal in the previous verse. If his readers knew he was hoping to see them soon, perhaps they would recognize his tender concern for them and be more inclined to respond to his message quickly.

Even though this verse names Timothy, it offers no definite clue as to the identity of the author. Many in the first-century church knew Timothy. (See Acts 17:14; 18:5.)

Timothy may have been arrested under Nero in Rome, then released at Nero's death. If so, the date of the letter would be in the late 60s.[105]

Verse 24. Here is the third reference to spiritual leaders in chapter 13. (See verses 7, 17.) The letter does not have spiritual leaders as it primary audience. They were not the ones tempted to revert to Judaism. Instead, the letter was written to the community of believers themselves. The author wished them to greet their spiritual leaders and all the saints on his behalf.

The word "saints" is translated from *hagious*, which implies "holiness." It is important to note that this word, a form of which is translated "sanctify," has to do primarily with separation. The Hebrew background of the word (*qadosh*) involves first the way God Himself was separate from His creation and then the way His chosen people, the Jews, were separated from the nations around them by the law of Moses. Only by association did the word begin to take on implications of morality. When we think of the word "holy," we tend to think immediately of the moral aspects of the word. But a person could choose to be a strict, uncompromising moralist, and yet if he had no faith in God he would not be holy. Because we have faith in God, we *are* holy; it is our faith that separates us from the unbelieving world around us. Genuine faith will produce results, and these results will include morality. But it is not morality that makes us holy; it is faith.

The phrase "they of Italy salute you" does not clearly reveal whether it refers to believers who formerly lived in Italy but now lived abroad, which could imply they were sending greetings back to Italy, or to believers who currently lived in Italy and were sending their greetings abroad. In the latter case, which would seem more likely if Timothy was imprisoned in Rome and now released, the letter would probably have been written from Rome.

Verse 25. The author's final wish was in harmony with that of many other New Testament letters: he wished for the grace of God to be with the believers to whom he wrote.[106] (For a discussion of the perspective of Hebrews on grace, see the comments on 2:9; 4:16; 10:29; 12:15, 28; 13:9.) In the final analysis, grace characterizes the new covenant (John 1:17; Ephesians 2:8-9), so there could be no more appropriate wish than desiring the grace of God.

Notes

[1]It may be somewhat surprising to know that Scripture does not explicitly give the measurements of the Holy Place and the Most Holy Place (also called the Holy of Holies or the Holiest of All). The common consensus is that the Holy Place was twenty cubits long by ten cubits high by ten cubits wide and that the Most Holy Place was ten cubits squared. The following facts support this conclusion:

1. The boards that stood upright forming the sides of the Tabernacle were ten cubits in length, making the Tabernacle height ten cubits (Exodus 26:16).

2. Each side of the Tabernacle was made up of twenty of these boards, each of which were a cubit and a half wide (Exodus 26:16-21).

3. The width of the Tabernacle was approximately ten cubits, for the west end of the Tabernacle consisted of six boards a cubit and a half wide (Exodus 26:22). These six boards placed side by side would measure nine cubits. There is some uncertainty here because there were two additional boards, each a cubit and a half wide, forming "the two back corners of the Tabernacle" (Exodus 26:23, NKJV). They were joined together with the adjacent boards to form the corners, making a total of eight boards across the west end (Exodus 26:24-25). We do not know exactly how they were positioned to form the corners.

4. The Tabernacle covering was a linen curtain consisting of ten smaller curtains joined together. Each of these ten curtains was twenty-eight cubits long and four cubits wide. When joined together, the resulting curtain was thus twenty-eight cubits by forty cubits. The curtains

were joined in such a way that precisely in the center, the fifth and sixth smaller curtains were joined with fifty "loops of blue yarn on the edge" of each curtain and "fifty clasps of gold" securing the curtains together. (See Exodus 26:1-6.) The finished product was twenty-eight cubits wide and forty cubits long. If the linen curtain was laid on the top of the Tabernacle framework beginning at the front (east) entrance, thirty cubits would be taken up to cover the top, leaving ten cubits to cover the back, or west, end behind the Most Holy Place. At precisely twenty cubits from the entrance and ten cubits from the west end, the elaborate loops of blue yarn connected by gold clasps would be visible on the ceiling. Since the linen curtain was twenty-eight cubits wide, and approximately ten cubits were needed to cover the width of the Tabernacle, approximately nine cubits would remain to hang down on both the north and south sides. This length would enclose the Tabernacle almost, but not quite, to the ground, since the height of the Tabernacle was ten cubits.

5. On top of the linen covering was a curtain of goats' hair. (See Exodus 26:7-13.) This curtain consisted of eleven smaller curtains, each thirty cubits long and four cubits wide. Thus the final curtain was thirty cubits wide and forty-four cubits long. The fifth and sixth curtains were joined by fifty loops on the edge of each curtain; each of the matching loops were fastened together by a bronze clasp. In its final form, the goats'-hair curtain was four cubits longer than the linen curtain. Since the extra four cubits were doubled and hung over the entrance to the Tabernacle, precisely forty cubits were left to cover the Tabernacle in the same way as the linen curtain. Thus, twenty cubits from the entrance and ten cubits from the

back of the Tabernacle, the goats'-hair curtain was joined by the bronze clasps exactly over the spot where the linen curtain was joined by the gold clasps. Westward beyond the clasps, the goats'-hair curtain extended another ten cubits over the top of the Tabernacle, then hung down ten cubits to cover the back. The goats'-hair curtain was thirty cubits wide, two cubits wider than the linen curtain, so with ten cubits taken up with covering the width of the Tabernacle, twenty cubits remained—ten on each side—to cover the sides of the Tabernacle all the way to the ground. From within the Tabernacle, then, approximately one cubit of the goats'-hair curtain was visible extending down beyond the linen curtain on both sides.

6. It seems reasonable that the veil which divided the Holy Place from the Most Holy Place would have hung down directly beneath the place where the linen curtain was joined by the blue loops and gold clasps. Hanging "the veil from the clasps" (Exodus 26:33, NKJV) may refer to the gold clasps that joined the linen curtain. Otherwise, there seems little reason for the linen and goats' hair curtains to be joined in this manner at precisely this place. There may be a clue here in the statements that the linen curtains are to be joined in this way "that it may be one Tabernacle" (Exodus 26:6) and that the goats' hair is also to be joined in this manner to "couple the tent together, that it may be one" (Exodus 26:11, NKJV). There is a recognition here that, in a sense, there are two tents, one holier than the other, but that in another sense, the two are one. As support of this view, Hebrews 9:2 indicates there was a first Tabernacle, the Holy Place, while Hebrews 9:3 points out that there was another Tabernacle, "the Holiest of all" (KJV).

[2]See previous note.

[3]Bruce M. Metzger, *A Textual Commentary on the Greek New Testament* (Stuttgart, Germany: United Bible Societies, 1971), 667.

[4]See discussion in F. F. Bruce, *The Epistle to the Hebrews*, in *The New International Commentary on the New Testament* (Grand Rapids, MI: Wm. B. Eerdmans Publishing Co., 1964), 184-85, and see discussion in Brooke Foss Westcott, *The Epistle to the Hebrews* (Repr., Grand Rapids, MI: Wm. B. Eerdmans Publishing Co., 1980), 246-47.

[5]See discussion in H. Orton Wiley, *The Epistle to the Hebrews* (Kansas City, MO: Beacon Hill Press, 1959), 282, and in John MacArthur, Jr., *Hebrews* (Chicago: Moody Press, 1983), 222-23.

[6]The Hebrew words commonly translated "showbread" are *lechem happanim*, which literally mean "bread of the face," signifying that it was bread set out before the face of God, or bread "shown" to Him. (See Bruce, 183, n. 12.)

[7]Walter A. Elwell, ed., *Baker Encyclopedia of the Bible* (Grand Rapids, MI: Baker Book House, 1988), 2:2016.

[8]See discussion on verse 2.

[9]See discussion in Paul Ellingworth, *Commentary on Hebrews*, in *New International Greek Testament Commentary* (Grand Rapids, MI: Wm. B. Eerdmans Publishing Co., 1993), 425-27, and see discussion in Bruce, 184-87.

[10]Elwell, 2:2016.

[11]See MacArthur, 222, and C.I. Scofield, ed., *The New Scofield Study Bible* (Nashville, TN: Thomas Nelson Publishers, 1989), 115, n. 2.

[12]The function of cherubim is apparently to protect and guard what God reserves to Himself. (See Genesis 3:24.)

[13]Ellingworth, 427.

[14]See Leon Morris, in Frank E. Gaebelein, gen. ed., *The Expositor's Bible Commentary* (Grand Rapids, MI: Zondervan Publishing House, 1981), 12:83.

[15]Ibid.

[16]Ellingworth, 444.

[17]Metzger, 668.

[18]A. T. Robertson, *Word Pictures in the New Testament* (Grand Rapids, MI: Baker Book House, 1932) 5:398.

[19]Jerry M. Hullinger, "The Problem of Animal Sacrifices in Ezekiel 40-48," *Bibliotheca Sacra* 152 (1995): 288.

[20]Zane C. Hodges, in John F. Walvoord and Roy B. Zuck, eds., *The Bible Knowledge Commentary*, New Testament edition (Wheaton, IL: Victor Books, 1983), 802.

[21]Bruce, 205.

[22]In *Dake's Annotated Reference Bible*, Finis Dake declared that God is three *separate* persons, but traditional trinitarianism says only that God is three *distinct* persons.

[23]Hullinger, 288.

[24]See Matthew 19:16; 19:29; 24:46; Mark 10:30; John 3:15-16, 36; 4:14, 36; 5:24, 39; 6:27, 40, 47, 54, 68; 10:28; 12:25, 50; 17:2-3; Acts 13:46, 48; Romans 2:7; 5:21; 6:22-23; Galatians 6:8; I Timothy 1:16; 6:12, 19; Titus 1:2; 3:7; I John 1:2; 2:25; 3:15; 5:11, 13, 20; Jude 1:21.

[25]Some people object to this view by citing the account of the rich young ruler (Matthew 19:16-26; Mark 10:17-27; Luke 18:18-27). They suppose that when Jesus called the young ruler's attention to the commandments of the law of Moses, He was instructing him to obey the law by faith, which would result in eternal life. But a comparison of each of the three accounts indicates otherwise.

First, though the young ruler said he had kept the commandments, he had no assurance of eternal life. If the law of Moses had promised eternal life on the basis of adherence to its commandments, it would seem reasonable to think that this young ruler would have been assured by his obedience.

Second, Jesus did not respond directly to his question. Instead, Jesus asked, "Why do you call Me good? No one is good but One, that is, God" (Matthew 19:17, NKJV). Jesus apparently was soliciting the young ruler's opinion as to His identity. Since only God is good, why did the young ruler call Jesus "good"? Did he recognize Jesus' claim to deity? If the young ruler recognized that Jesus was no mere man, but God manifest in flesh, he was well on his way to receiving the gift of eternal life. Apparently, however, the young ruler did not understand this. There is no record of any response to Jesus' question.

Third, Jesus responded to the young ruler's question on the basis of the law of Moses, which was still in effect. He said, "But if you want to enter into life, keep the commandments" (Matthew 19:17, NKJV). We may *assume* here that when Jesus referred to "life," He had eternal life in view, but that is an assumption. It is significant that only Matthew records this statement. Matthew was written to a Jewish audience, and the Jewish people knew the promise of life as it was found in the law of Moses. Jesus did not ignore the young ruler's failure to grasp His identity and then commend the keeping of the law of Moses as a way to gain eternal life. Rather, because of the young ruler's lack of perception, Jesus resorted to the law of Moses, the lesser revelation under which the young ruler still labored. Otherwise, Jesus is made to offer eternal life on the basis of the mere keeping of the law of Moses, even apart from belief on Him.

Fourth, the young ruler stated that he had kept the commandments from his youth. But he still had not attained eternal life. Jesus responded to the young ruler's claim by saying, "One thing you lack" (Mark 10:21, NKJV). In other words, in spite of the young ruler's adherence to the law of Moses, he had not attained eternal life. The one requirement for eternal life was still lacking.

Fifth, it was not by selling his goods and giving to the poor that the young ruler would attain eternal life, but by following Jesus, which, by implication, means believing on Jesus. It would have been possible for the young ruler to sell all and give to the poor without following Jesus; there would have been no eternal life in that. We know that the real issue was faith in Christ, not only because He said, "Take up the cross, and follow me" (Mark 10:21, NKJV), but also because Jesus explained to His amazed disciples, "How hard it is for those who trust in riches to enter the kingdom of God" (Mark 10:24, NKJV).

The young man trusted in his riches rather than trusting in God, and that was precisely his problem. The only way he could have received eternal life was by trusting in God, which implicitly meant believing on Jesus, not merely by the commandments of the law of Moses, which he kept anyway. As Tuck has pointed out, "The intended message is that the young man was not vindicated by his 'faithfulness' toward the Ten Commandments; rather he was indicted for his faithlessness toward the Messiah who was indicated by and superseded Moses. The regular New Testament thought is that rejection of Messiah in favor of Moses demonstrates actual unfaithfulness even toward Moses (cf. Luke 16:31; John 5:39-47; Rom. 9:31-10:4)." Gary Earl Tuck, "The Purpose of the Law Relative to Sin in Pauline Literature," Th.D. dissertation, Dallas Theological Seminary, 1991: 96.

[26]See discussion in Bruce, 216.

[27]David J. MacLeod, "The Cleansing of the True Tabernacle," *Bibliotheca Sacra* 152 (January–March 1995): 61.

[28]Ibid., 71.

[29]See Morris, 91, and Ellingworth, 478.

[30]Ellingworth, 487.

[31]See Morris, 93.

[32]Hodges, 803.

[33]Bruce, 232.

[34]Ellingworth, 500.

[35]Ibid.

[36]In Philippians 2:6, the word "form" (Greek, *morphe*) has to do with an external appearance that is truly indicative of the essence of a thing. The word "being" (Greek, *hyparchon*) is a participle, which indicates continual existence. The word translated "robbery" (Greek, *harpagmon*) is somewhat of a puzzle, since it appears only here in New Testament Greek, nowhere in the Septuagint, and rarely in secular Greek. The idea of *harpagmon* seems to

be "a prize to be grasped," whether already possessed or yet future, or as suggested in a marginal note in the *New Scofield Study Bible*, "a thing to be held on to." In both appearances of the word "God" in this verse (Greek, *theos*), it is without the definite article, which usually indicates divine essence rather than emphasizing the person of God. Thus, the verse seems to mean that before the Incarnation, He who became incarnate existed continually in His divine essence, including the external "appearance" of that essence (which would presumably have been revealed only to the angels, who are spirit beings, since God is invisible), but He did not consider this "appearance" something to retain as He contemplated adding human existence to His existence as God. Thus, what He gave up in the Incarnation was not deity, but the appearance of deity.

[37]Walter Bauer, *A Greek-English Lexicon of the New Testament and Other Early Christian Literature*, trans. William F. Arndt and F. Wilbur Gingrich, rev. F. Wilbur Gingrich and Frederick W. Danker, 2nd ed. (Chicago: University of Chicago Press, 1979), 877.

[38]See discussion in Bruce, 233-34.

[39]Here is an overview of various theories of the Atonement:

The Ransom Theory. Later theologians have called this the classical theory because of its widespread acceptance in the first millennium of Christianity. Origen and Gregory of Nyssa were among those who developed this view.

This theory of the Atonement holds that Satan was in legal possession of the souls of people because of their sins. God made an agreement with Satan to trade the soul of the sinless Jesus for the souls of all those who would accept Jesus as their Savior. Since the soul of Jesus was the only one not legally belonging to Satan, this offer was attractive to Satan. He did not realize, however, that Jesus was actually the Son of God. So when Jesus died and Satan attempted to possess His soul, he discovered much to his surprise and dismay that he could not hold the soul of Jesus. Jesus was too powerful for Satan to hold, and thus Satan had neither the soul of Jesus nor the souls of those who accepted Jesus.

The ransom or devil ransom theory has also been called the fishhook theory because some of the early church writers described it in terms of a fisherman who places an attractive bait over the hook in order to attract the fish. The humanity of Jesus was the bait over the hook of deity. When Satan "bit" the humanity, he discovered too late the deity.

While this theory sounds crude and implies deception on God's part, we should recognize that there is an element of truth in it. That is, in the Atonement God did gain a marvelous victory over Satan, a victory that Satan doubtless did not anticipate. (See I Corinthians 2:8; Colossian 2:15.)

The Satisfaction Theory. In the eleventh century Anselm, archbishop of Canterbury, suggested a view of the Atonement known as the commercial or satisfaction theory. It sees the Atonement as compensation to the Father for His honor wounded by the sins of humanity. Anselm saw sin as essentially failure to give God what is due Him. Since he also pictured God as a feudal overlord who, to maintain his honor, insists that there be adequate satisfaction for any encroachment upon it, Anselm

believed that God's violated honor could be put right
again only in one of two ways. Either He must punish or
condemn those who have violated His honor, or He could
accept satisfaction made in behalf of those who have violated His honor. Sinful humans could not make adequate
payment, for regardless of what they did, they would only
be giving God what was already due Him. Therefore, a
greater compensation was required, which made the
Incarnation logically necessary. Since Christ was both
God and man, the value of His life was infinite, and since
He was sinless and did not deserve punishment, His offering of His own life went beyond what could have been
required of Him. Thus God was able to accept the death
of Jesus as payment for His offended honor.

While Anselm's theory reflected the political milieu of
his day and suggested that God was somewhat like a feudal lord who feared his serfs might become unruly if he
did not deal with them firmly, it did emphasize the seriousness of sin and the costliness of forgiveness.

The Moral Influence Theory. Also in the eleventh
century, Peter Abelard presented another view of the
Atonement, largely in response to Anselm. Abelard, a
scholastic philosopher, taught that forgiveness was not
impossible as far as God was concerned. The only problem was that God could offer forgiveness only to those
who requested it. The essential need, then, was not for
some price to be paid either to Satan or God, but for
humans to be influenced to repent.

In order to bring humans to see their need of repentance, God sent His Son to suffer and die for man as a
manifestation of divine love. When they saw the great sacrifice God had made, they would be moved to shame and

repentance, thus enabling God to forgive them.

While there is some truth in this view, in that the Cross is without question an unsurpassable demonstration of the love of God (John 3:16; I John 4:9-10; Romans 5:8), Abelard was condemned for heresy. The reason is that this view indicates Christ did not make any sort of sacrificial payment to the Father; He merely demonstrated His love for man. Thus the Cross was for man's benefit only. It was a piece of divine showmanship and nothing more.

The church did not see how a death that did not actually accomplish something could be a demonstration of love. As an illustration, let us suppose Jones and Smith are walking along a river and Jones, who is unable to swim, falls into the water. If Smith jumps in to save Jones, we can interpret his efforts as love. But if Jones does not fall into the river and Smith jumps into the water anyway, flailing about while shouting, "See how much I love you!" we would not interpret Smith's actions as a demonstration of love but of questionable sanity. Jones will not be moved to love Smith but to pity him. If the death of Jesus Christ does not actually reconcile us to God, it would seem to be merely a cosmic drama where God, like Smith, does something totally unnecessary in an attempt to impress humans with His love.

The Socinian Theory. A sixteenth-century theory explained the Atonement as merely providing an example people should follow in their total and selfless devotion to God. This teaching, developed by Faustus and Laelius Socinus, rejected any idea of vicarious satisfaction.

This view, most fully expressed by Unitarians, holds to a Pelagian view of the human condition. (Pelagius taught that people are not sinners by nature, that Adam's sin affected only Adam, and that all people have the ability to do God's will and to fulfill His expectations by their own power.) Since people have the total power of choice over each decision, all they need is an example to follow. The death of Christ provided that example.

The Socinian theory also holds that God is not a God of retribution and that He does not demand any form of payment or satisfaction from those who have offended Him. It sees Jesus as a mere human who was able to surrender perfectly to God.

The Socinian view overlooks the many passages of Scripture that describe the death of Jesus as a ransom, a sacrifice, a case of sin bearing, and a practice of priesthood, focusing instead on I Peter 2:21: "For even hereunto were ye called: because Christ also suffered for us, leaving us an example, that ye should follow his steps." The idea is that we are called to suffer as Christ suffered. The context of this verse, however, sees the death of Christ as sin bearing: "Who his own self bare our sins in his own body on the tree, that we, being dead to sins, should live unto righteousness: by whose stripes ye were healed" (I Peter 2:24). Our suffering is limited to the willing acceptance of undeserved wrongs: "For this is thankworthy, if a man for conscience toward God endure grief, suffering wrongfully. For what glory is it, if, when ye be buffeted for your faults, ye shall take it patiently? but if, when ye do well, and suffer for it, ye take it patiently, this is acceptable with God" (I Peter 2:19-20).

The Governmental Theory. This theory describes the Atonement as a demonstration of divine justice. It views sin as a serious wrong that demands justice on a scale corresponding to the magnitude of the infraction.

Whereas some atonement theories are almost purely objective (viewing the Atonement as affecting God only, usually in satisfying His divine displeasure with sin) and others are almost purely subjective (viewing the Atonement as affecting humans only, usually in impressing on them the gravity of sin or the love of God), the governmental theory is a mediating view with both objective and subjective elements.

Hugo Grotius, a late sixteenth- and early seventeenth-century Calvinist who later embraced Arminianism, developed this view in response to the Socinian theory. According to Grotius, God is a holy and righteous ruler who has established laws that must be obeyed. If they are disobeyed, God has the right to punish the offender. Since God is a God of love, however, He can make a sovereign choice to forgive sin and absolve humans of guilt. But since He also must keep in mind the importance of demonstrating the obligation of humans to keep His law, He chose to deal with human guilt in a way that would demonstrate both His clemency and severity.

Grotius saw God as a ruler rather as a creditor or master. Whereas a creditor may cancel a debt if he chooses, and a master may punish or refrain from punishing his servants, a ruler cannot simply overlook the laws of his realm. Grotius described the death of Christ as an act of "penal substitution." Instead of Christ taking the penalty of death that should have been inflicted on the human race, the death of Christ was a substitution for a penalty. Grotius did not believe it was possible to transfer a penalty from one person to another, so his view differed from that of Anselm, who saw the Atonement as a penalty inflicted on Christ instead of on human beings.

According to Grotius, then, the suffering of Christ was not a vicarious bearing of the sins of others, but a demonstration of God's hatred of sin that, when viewed by the human race, would induce them to understand the horror of sin and turn from it. As they turned in repentance, they could receive forgiveness.

Grotius' theory differed from Socianism in that he saw the death of Christ as more than a beautiful example of how Christians should live; he saw in the Atonement an illustration of the consequences of sin. Grotius believed that people not only had to be encouraged to do good, they must be deterred from doing evil.

The governmental theory differs from the moral influence theory in that the former sees the death of Christ as a legitimate offering made to God by Christ, upon the basis of which God is able to deal mercifully with humanity. This is the objective element in the theory. But the main emphasis of Grotius' view is its subjective element: the impression made upon humans of the seriousness of sin and its consequences.

Other Views. In addition to these theories of the Atonement, other views with sometimes subtle differences from the above have surfaced in church history.

The Recapitulation Theory. While this view contains the idea that Christ was a ransom to Satan, it goes beyond the ransom theory to suggest that Christ in His life and death repeated all the stages of human life that belong to humans as sinners, including death. By doing so, Christ replaced Adam's disobedience with obedience. This obedience becomes humanity's by faith and accomplishes an ethical transformation. Irenaeus (c. 130-200) suggested this view.

The Dramatic Theory. Aulen (1930) suggested that the Atonement was actually a divine drama illustrating the struggle between evil and good and presenting Christ as the ultimate victor in the conflict.

The Mystical Theory. This view, represented by Schleiermacher (d. 1834), says Jesus took on a sinful human nature but successfully triumphed over it by the power of the Holy Spirit. Rather than salvation lying in the cross of Christ, it rests in His person. His divine-human nature is communicable to humans, and therein lies salvation.

The Vicarious Repentance Theory. According to this view, put forth by John McLeod Campbell (d. 1872), all that humans need to obtain forgiveness is an adequate repentance. Since humans are unable to repent sufficiently, Christ acted on their behalf, meeting the conditions for forgiveness. Christ's death also stimulates humans to the life of holiness necessary for acceptance by God.

[40]Ellingworth, 518.

[41]See discussion in Daniel L. Segraves, *Themes from a Letter to Rome* (Hazelwood, MO: Word Aflame Press, 1995), 134-36.

[42]Ellingworth, 526.

[43]See Daniel L. Segraves, *James: Faith at Work* (Hazelwood, MO: Word Aflame Press, 1995).

[44]Bruce, 262.

[45]See discussion in Bruce, 267.

[46]Ibid., 270.

[47]Ibid., 268.

[48]See comments in volume 1 on *hypostasis* in 1:3. In that case, it has an objective meaning, indicating that Christ is the essence of God. But in 3:14 and 11:1, the

word is better understood in the subjective sense of assurance. (See discussion in Morris, 113, and Bruce, 278.)

[49]See discussion in Bruce, 283-86.

[50]Bruce, 283.

[51]Ibid., 284.

[52]Craig S. Keener, *The Bible Background Commentary, New Testament* (Downers Grove, IL: InterVarsity Press, 1993), 532.

[53]Ibid., 675.

[54]Morris, 119.

[55]Ibid.

[56]Bruce, 297, n. 85.

[57]See Bruce, 312.

[58]Bruce, 317-18.

[59]Ibid., 318, n. 176.

[60]Ibid., 317, n. 175.

[61]The KJV translation of Acts 7:20, which has Moses being "exceeding fair," does not completely translate the Greek *asteios toi theoi*.

[62]Morris, 126.

[63]Ibid.

[64]Bruce, 322, n. 194.

[65]Ibid., 323.

[66]See Bruce, 321-23, both text and notes, for a discussion of these efforts to reconcile the accounts in Exodus and Hebrews. Leon Morris, in Morris, *The Expositor's Bible Commentary*, notes the difficulty in reconciling the accounts and gives supporting evidence for both the exit to Midian and the Exodus. Morris prefers the flight to Midian as the occasion in view, but he makes no attempt to reconcile the reference to Moses' lack of fear in Hebrews to the record of his fear in Exodus.

[67]See, for example, the flight of Joseph, Mary and Jesus into Egypt to escape Herod's wrath (Matthew 2:13-15) and Paul's escape from Damascus in a basket by night (Acts 9:23-25; II Corinthians 11:32-33). Neither was an act of fear or cowardice.

[68]Bruce, 337.

[69]Ibid.

[70]Ibid., 340-41.

[71]The critical text omits the words "were tempted."

[72]Robertson, 432.

[73]Morris, 133.

[74]Robertson, 432.

[75]Ibid.

[76]Ibid.; Morris, 134; Keener, 678.

[77]William Barclay, *The Making of the Bible* (New York: Abingdon Press, 1961), 13-14.

[78]Morris, 134.

[79]Robertson, 433.

[80]Bruce, 355, n. 51.

[81]See discussion in Bruce, xliiff. and 266ff.

[82]A topic of debate in the area of biblical anthropology has been the origin of the soul or spirit in all humans after Adam and Eve. According to the *creationist* view, God creates each spirit and places it in the human being at conception. Under the *preexistent* view, God created all souls or spirits at some point in eternity, later assigning each one to a body. This view is pagan in origin. The *traducian* position says the immaterial nature is communicated to the child by his parents in the process of conception, along with the physical body.

The creation of the original man is distinct from the creation of all else, for the Lord God "breathed into his nostrils the breath of life; and man became a living soul" (Genesis 2:7). Thus the immaterial part of Adam originated directly with the breath of God. But what is the origin of the soul in people descended from Adam?

We must reject the idea that souls are preexistent, waiting to be assigned to bodies, as lacking biblical evidence. Eastern religions have accepted the idea of the "transmigration of the soul," but this view—which would allow the possibility of reincarnation—is without scriptural support.

While some theologians have endorsed and continue to support the theory that God creates a new soul for each child born, it raises several problems. One has to do with the impact of this idea on the doctrine of the original sin. How would sin then be imputed to the human race? Does God create sinful souls? Or does He create innocent or holy souls but infuse them with sin at some point after they are assigned to a body? And when do the soul and the body unite? Is it ever possible for there to be a baby in the womb with no soul?

The traducian theory seems more in keeping with the biblical witness and the observable facts. Just as Adam was made in the image and likeness of God, he "begat a son in his own likeness, after his image; and called his name Seth" (Genesis 5:3). If the image of God in Adam included his immaterial nature, it would seem that the image of Adam in Seth would include the same. When God gave humans the command and ability to multiply and replenish the earth (Genesis 1:28), He did not limit that reproductive ability to the physical body. It was the ability to authentically reproduce humanity, including both the material and immaterial parts. This view eliminates the problem of God creating sinful souls, it explains the communication of the sinful nature to all humanity from our father Adam, and it fits with the observable facts of psychology.

[83]See the discussion on sickness as divine discipline in Segraves, *James: Faith at Work*, 189-91.

[84]See "Holiness: Separating unto God and from Sin" in Segraves, *Themes from a Letter to Rome*, 173-204.

[85]See "Righteousness and Justification: Imputing Right Standing to the Believer's Account" in Segraves, *Themes from a Letter to Rome*, 11-61.

[86]See discussion in H. E. Dana and Julius R. Mantey, *A Manual Grammar of the Greek New Testament* (New York: Macmillan Publishing Co., Inc., 1955), 250-51.

[87]See Bruce, 367.

[88]Ibid., 366.

[89]See discussion in Ellingworth, 668.

[90]Morris, 140.

[91]Westcott, 408.

[92]See discussion in Bruce, 373.

[93]See discussion of the typological function of Jewish history in Bruce, 62-63.

[94]See Matthew 19:16, 29; 24:46; Mark 10:30; John 3:15-16, 36; 4:14, 36; 5:24, 39; 6:27, 40, 47, 54, 68; 10:28; 12:25, 50; 17:2-3; Acts 13:46, 48; Romans 2:7; 5:21; 6:22-23; Galatians 6:8; I Timothy 1:16; 6:12, 19; Titus 1:2; 3:7; I John 1:2; 2:25; 3:15; 5:11, 13, 20; Jude 1:21.

[95]Bruce, 381, n. 193.

[96]Bauer, 861.

[97]Ellingworth, 694.

[98]Ibid.

[99]Bruce, 390.

[100]See discussion in Bruce, 392, and Ellingworth, 696.

[101]See discussion in Bruce, 392.

[102]See discussion in Ellingworth, 697.

[103]See discussion in Bruce, 399-402.

[104]In the Hebrew Scriptures, the phrase "an everlasting covenant" is used in connection with the Abrahamic covenant (Genesis 17:7, 13, 19; I Chronicles 16:17; Psalm 105:10), the Mosaic covenant (Leviticus 24:8), the Davidic covenant (II Samuel 23:5), and the new covenant (Isaiah 55:3; 61:8; Jeremiah 32:40; Ezekiel 16:60; 37:26). The phrase "the everlasting covenant" is used in connection with the Noahic covenant (Genesis 9:16) and the Mosaic covenant (Isaiah 24:5).

[105]Keener, 684-85.

[106]See I Corinthians 16:23; II Corinthians 13:14; Galatians 6:18; Ephesians 6:24; Philippians 4:23; Colossians 4:18; I Thessalonians 5:28; II Thessalonians 3:18; I Timothy 6:21; II Timothy 4:22; Titus 3:15; Philemon 25; II Peter 3:18; Revelation 22:21.